THE YOUNG OXFORD LIBRARY OF SCIENCE

Electricity and Electronics

Paul Marks

OXFORD
UNIVERSITY PRESS

Great Clarendon Street, Oxford OX2 6DP

Oxford University Press is a department of the University of Oxford.
It furthers the University's objective of excellence in research, scholarship,
and education by publishing worldwide in

Oxford New York

Auckland Bangkok Buenos Aires Cape Town Chennai
Dar es Salaam Delhi Hong Kong Istanbul Karachi
Kolkata Kuala Lumpur Madrid Melbourne Mexico City Mumbai
Nairobi São Paulo Shanghai Singapore Taipei Tokyo Toronto

with an associated company in Berlin

Oxford is a registered trade mark of Oxford University Press
in the UK and in certain other countries

British Library Cataloguing in Publication Data available

Hardback ISBN 0-19-910936-2
Paperback ISBN 0-19-910937-0

1 3 5 7 9 10 8 6 4 2

Designed and typeset by Full Steam Ahead
Printed in Malaysia.

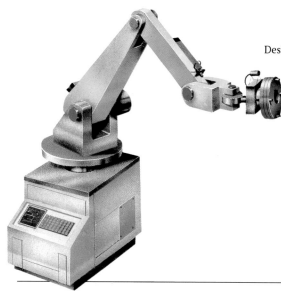

CONTENTS

HARNESSING SPARKS

Blasting out of the sky like a jagged laser beam, a bolt of lightning strikes a tree, scorching it to a blackened crisp. The power of a lightning strike is spectacular and dangerous. What is this strange, violent energy that comes from the sky?

The answer is that lightning is a form of electricity. During a thunderstorm, clouds can store up electricity. When enough electricity has built up, it zaps between the clouds and the ground in the form of a lightning strike.

Electric power

Lightning is one way in which electricity occurs in nature. But it's man-made electricity that powers much of today's world. Without it, we would have no commonplace gadgets such as personal stereos, computers, televisions, toasters, programmable dishwashers and mobile phones. So what exactly is this stuff called electricity that we all depend on so much?

Charging about

All substances are made of tiny particles called atoms. In the middle of each atom

▼ Lightning over a city. Metal rods called lightning conductors, mounted high on buildings, have been used for hundreds of years to help lightning strikes leak harmlessly to earth.

FRANKLIN'S EXPERIMENT
In 1752, the American statesman and inventor Ben Franklin (1706–1790) undertook a very risky experiment. He flew a kite with a salty thread (which electricity could flow through) near thunderclouds. He managed to get electric current to leak down the thread to charge a Leyden jar – a very early form of battery. This proved that lightning was another form of electricity. Others who tried to copy Franklin's experiment were not so lucky – at least two were struck by lightning and killed.

there is a core called a nucleus. Around this nucleus is a cloud of very light particles called electrons. Electricity results from the behaviour of the electrons, which possess a strange property called electric charge.

No-one knows exactly what electric charge is, but we know there are two kinds: positive and negative. Electrons have a

(a)

electrostatic charge

drum

(b)

light beam

lamp

charge remains in dark area

(c)

toner

(d)

toner transferred to paper

(e)

heated rollers fix image

USING STATIC TO MAKE COPIES

Static electricity plays an important part in the photocopying process. First, a drum inside the photocopier is charged with static electricity (a). Then light is shone on the image being copied. The light reflects onto the drum, and in the bright areas it makes the drum lose charge (b). There is now a pattern of charge on the drum, a copy of the pattern of light and dark on the original image. An ink powder called toner is now spread on the drum, but it only sticks to the charged areas (c). This toner pattern is then transferred from the drum to a piece of paper (d) and fixed by two heated rollers (e).

negative charge. They are attracted towards positive charges (the nucleus of an atom is positively charged) and forced away from, or repelled, by other negative charges.

Atoms have a balance of electric charge, because the positive charges in the nucleus balance out the negative charges of the electrons. But some substances can accept extra electrons, while others lose electrons quite easily. So objects can become electrically charged. This is known as static electricity. Charge cannot build up on materials such as metals because they let electrons flow through them. We call a flow of electric charge 'current electricity'.

Passing on the charge

If you have ever received a small electric shock after walking across a thick carpet and grasping a metal door handle, you will have experienced the effects of static electricity. Static electricity will also make a balloon stick to the wall after you have rubbed it on your hair.

In static electricity, electrons create a stationary charge. For example, when you rub the balloon on your hair, loosely held electrons in your hair are rubbed off on to the balloon. The object that loses the

● key words

- atom
- charge
- current
- electron
- static electricity

▶ The charge on a balloon can make your hair stand on end.

electrons (your hair) builds up a positive charge, while the object that gains the electrons (the balloon) builds up a negative charge. The balloon will then stick to the wall because its negative charges are attracted to positive charges in the wall. Similarly, when you walk across a fluffy carpet, loose electrons in the carpet hop on to your body, charging you up. You don't feel this until you grab a metal door handle. Then the electron charge is released into the metal through your hand, and you feel a small shock. You may also hear a crackle, as this electricity makes a spark as it jumps to the metal.

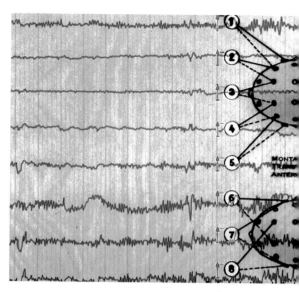

▶ Doctors use the electrical signals made by the brain to find out whether people have certain illnesses.

Interestingly, lightning involves both static and current electricity. During a storm, electrons build up inside the lower surface of clouds to make a static electric charge. When the attraction between the negatively charged cloud and the positively charged ground (or even another cloud) is great enough, electrons flow through the air in a searing current that makes the air glow. This is what we call lightning.

Electricity and magnetism

Electricity is very closely related to magnetism. That's because both depend on the way electrons behave. A material can be magnetic if many of its electrons spin in the same direction. When an electric current moves through a wire, it also creates a magnetic field around it. And moving a wire through a magnetic field can produce an electric current in the wire. Both these effects are used in many of the electric machines that we use every day.

Current affairs

In current electricity, electrons are made to flow through a material such as a metal wire. A battery, or another power supply such as mains electricity, pushes electrons through the wires. This flow of electrons creates an electric current. As electric current passes through metal wires, it can power a light bulb, turn a motor or do many other useful jobs.

▲ The high electric current that flows through an electric arc-welder creates a high-temperature 'spark' that is hot enough to melt metal. It can be used to cut through pieces of metal or to join them together.

Our bodies are full of electricity. The 10 billion nerve cells in your brain work by sending messages in the form of bursts of electricity (impulses) to each other. Reading this page will have set off hundreds of impulses as your nerves sent messages from your eyes to your brain.

MOVING AND STOPPING ELECTRICITY

The ring of an electric cooker glows brightly when electricity is passing through it. But if the ring were made of wood instead of metal, it would not work. That's because some materials do not let electricity pass through them.

▶ These ceramic (pottery) insulators are placed between high-power electricity cables and the pylons that support them. They stop electricity from flowing into the pylon itself.

Materials that let electricity pass through them are called conductors. Materials that don't are called insulators.

key words
- conductor
- electron
- insulator
- semiconductor
- superconductor

Conductors

Conductors are usually made of metal, or at least mainly of metal. Silver and copper are two of the best conductors. Copper is most widely used for electrical wiring.

Metals are good conductors because they have many spare electrons (the tiny particles that move round atoms). These electrons are free to move. They can be made to move by a battery or by mains electricity. When electrons move, or flow, they create an electric current.

Insulators

Insulating materials such as concrete or rubber hold on tightly to their electrons, so the electrons are not free to move. Materials that resist the flow of electricity

▼ The small disc in this photo is a magnet. It is repelled so strongly by the superconductor below that it hovers in mid-air. New trains called maglevs use superconductors and magnets in this way to make the train hover above the track.

can be very useful. Wall sockets and plugs are made of thick plastic, which is a good insulator. This stops us from getting electric shocks.

Special conductors

Electrically, some materials are between conductors and insulators. Materials like this are called semiconductors. Silicon is the best known. Semiconductors can be treated with chemicals to change how well they conduct electricity.

Other materials called superconductors conduct electricity incredibly well at low temperatures. They are also strongly diamagnetic – they strongly repel magnets.

PORTABLE POWER

There's a car accident, and someone who saw the crash uses their mobile phone to call an ambulance. Minutes later, the injured are being rushed to hospital. The time saved by using a mobile phone could help to save their lives.

Portable gadgets like mobile phones and portable TVs can be extremely useful. But to be portable, they have to get their power from batteries. A battery is a clever collection of chemicals that can react together to make electricity.

Electrical chemistry

How does a battery release electrons? It does so through a carefully chosen pair of chemical reactions. A battery can have one or more parts, called cells. Each cell has two pieces of metal (the electrodes) dipped in a chemical called an electrolyte.

key words

- battery
- terminal
- cell
- electrode
- electrolyte

▼ Solar power. Out in space, satellites cannot be serviced or refuelled. Many of them rely on huge solar panels to generate the electricity they need to work.

BATTERY VARIETY

Different types of battery use different chemicals to produce electricity. A car has a powerful, rechargeable lead-acid battery (a). The electrodes are made of lead compounds, while the electrolyte is an acid. A personal stereo uses an alkaline battery (b). In this the electrodes are powders, mixed with an electrolyte to make a paste.

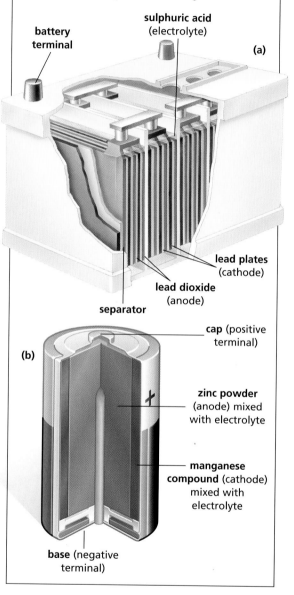

battery terminal

sulphuric acid (electrolyte)

(a)

lead plates (cathode)

lead dioxide (anode)

separator

cap (positive terminal)

(b)

zinc powder (anode) mixed with electrolyte

manganese compound (cathode) mixed with electrolyte

base (negative terminal)

When a battery is connected up, chemical reactions takes place between the electrodes and the electrolyte. At one electrode (the negative terminal or anode), there is a chemical reaction that produces electrons. These electrons can then flow as electricity. At the other electrode (the positive terminal or cathode), another chemical reaction uses up electrons.

Dissolving away

The chemical reactions that happen at the anode and the cathode of a battery affect the materials that they are made of. The anode slowly dissolves away, while the cathode becomes encrusted with chemicals. In some kinds of battery this process cannot be reversed, and the anode eventually wears out. This is what happens when a battery goes flat. But in a rechargeable battery, the chemical reactions that make the battery work can be reversed by connecting the battery up to an electricity supply and running it in reverse. This is what happens when you use a charger to recharge a battery.

▲ The electric motor that drives this experimental car is powered by a fuel cell instead of a battery.

GALVANI AND VOLTA

In 1791 an Italian anatomist called Luigi Galvani (1737–1798) was probing a dead frog's nerves with tools made of different metals. He noticed that when he did this, the frog's leg muscles twitched. Alessandro Volta (1745–1827) at the University of Pavia heard about Galvani's discovery. Volta worked out that the twitching was caused by electricity. The metal instruments were acting like electrodes in a battery, while the fluids in the frog's body were the electrolyte.

Alessandro Volta

This discovery inspired Volta to developed the voltaic pile, in 1799. The pile was a battery with a number of cells, each with one electrode of zinc and one of silver, with a layer of card soaked in salt water between them. This was the world's first-ever battery.

Volta's pile

Luigi Galvani

Solar cells and fuel cells

Batteries are not the only portable sources of electric power – solar cells and fuel cells can also make electricity.

A solar cell makes electricity using sunlight. Inside the cell are special materials that release electrons when they are bathed in light. Solar cells are used, for example, in space probes and satellites. At present they are not very efficient – they can only turn about 15 per cent of the light that falls on them into electrical energy. But scientists hope to make better solar cells in the future.

Fuel cells make electricity using hydrogen as a fuel. A chemical reaction in the fuel cell turns the hydrogen into water, at the same time producing electrons that can flow in a circuit. But hydrogen is difficult and dangerous to store, so engineers are now trying to make fuel cells safe. Fuel cells are more powerful than batteries, and scientists hope that they can soon be used to power cars. Tiny fuel cells may also be used to power personal stereos and tiny 'wearable' computers.

LOOPING THE LOOP

Have you ever wondered how flicking a switch on the wall can cause a light bulb to glow on the other side of the room, as if by magic? When you press the switch, a lever brings two pieces of metal together inside the switch. This opens a pathway for electric current to travel along – like lowering the drawbridge for people to enter a castle. Electricity gushes into the light bulb, making it burn brightly.

The path that the electric current flows along is called a circuit. A torch, for example, contains a simple circuit that has three components parts – a battery, a light bulb and a switch. These are joined together in a loop by strips of metal, which conduct electricity.

All electrical equipment and gadgets depend on circuits, which may have different components connected in different ways, depending on the job the piece of equipment does. Whether you are adding numbers on a calculator, watching TV or heating food in a microwave oven, an electric circuit is doing the work for you.

▶ A torch is an example of a very simple but very useful circuit. A bulb is connected to a battery and a switch. Pushing the switch on lets electrons travel, and the bulb lights up.

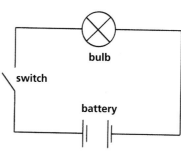

▲ This circuit diagram shows the torch circuit very simply, using symbols for the bulb, the battery and the switch.

reflector

bulb

positive terminal

switch

connection to bulb from negative terminal

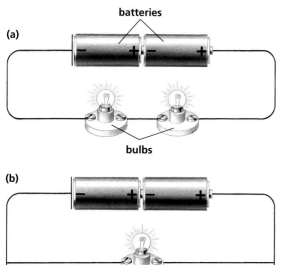

(a)
batteries
bulbs

(b)

◀ Two identical light bulbs connected in series (a) and in parallel (b). The bulbs in series glow more dimly because the current is reduced. Also, if one bulb breaks in the series circuit, the other goes out because the circuit is broken. In parallel, each bulb has its own circuit, so if one bulb blows, the other keeps working.

Going with the flow

All circuits need a supply of electricity. The supply will set electrons (tiny particles found in atoms) moving around the circuit.

Electrons carry an electric charge, so as they move they produce a flow of electricity called a current. Current is measured in amperes (amps). If there is a break in the circuit, the current will stop flowing. Electricity does not flow through a circuit by itself. It needs a 'push', or energy, to keep it moving. We call this energy the voltage of the circuit. Voltage is measured in volts (V).

The power used by a device is a measure of how fast it uses energy. Power is measured in watts (W). A bar of an electric fire uses about 1000 W.

Electric power can come either from a battery or from a mains socket. A battery produces direct current (DC): this means that the current flows one way around the circuit. Mains electricity is alternating current (AC). Alternating current flows first one way round the circuit, then the other, changing direction many times per second.

Resistance

Some electrical components reduce – or resist – the flow of current through a circuit. We say that they have a resistance. When a current flows through a light bulb, for example, the atoms in the bulb's filament – the coiled wire inside the bulb – resist the flow. This causes the atoms to get hot, making the filament glow. Resistance was discovered by Georg Ohm in 1826, and is measured in ohms.

Components called resistors are put into circuits to help control the flow of current through the circuit.

When there is a current of 1 ampere in a circuit, more than a million, million, million electrons flow through it every second.

OHM'S LAW

The German scientist Georg Ohm (1787–1854) is best remembered for working out Ohm's Law. He discovered that the voltage across a conductor – such as a strip of metal or a wire – and the current flowing through it, always vary in the same proportion. So if you double the voltage, you double the current. This is incredibly useful, because it lets you predict the current you will get for a particular voltage.

Series and parallel

If several bulbs (or other components) are powered by the same battery, they can be connected in series (in line) or in parallel. In parallel, each bulb is directly connected to the battery, so each gets the full voltage and glows brightly. If one bulb breaks, the others keep working. In series, the bulbs get less current and glow dimly. If one breaks, the others go out.

● **key words**
- battery
- circuit
- current
- resistance
- voltage

▼ Machines like TVs and radios have very complicated circuits with lots of parts. Instead of connecting all the parts with wires, the components are fastened to a circuit board, which has tiny silver tracks connecting them in the right order.

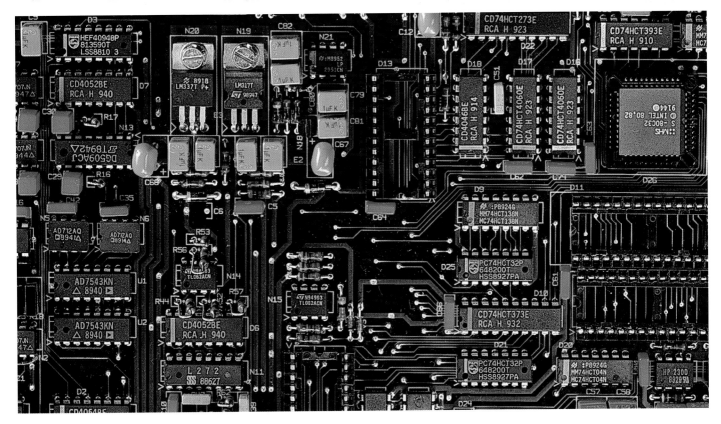

ATTRACTIVE OR REPULSIVE?

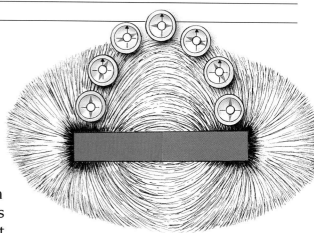

Without magnetism many things we take for granted today would not exist. The electricity that powers all the electrical items in your home, for example, comes from generators that use huge magnets to create electric current. And in your television, the picture is moved and changed many times each second by magnets inside the TV tube.

▲ If you scatter tiny iron filings around a magnet, they line up along the lines of magnetic force around the magnet. More filings collect at the poles than anywhere else. A compass needle will also point along the lines of magnetic force.

Magnetism is a force that is found in nature and has been known about for thousands of years. Before scientists discovered how it worked, it was thought to be a magical power. Magnetism is closely related to electricity and can do important work for us.

magnet

(a)

(b)

Quite repulsive

A magnet can attract other objects or repel other magnets (push them away) without touching them. All magnets are surrounded by an invisible magnetic field, where their magnetism can be felt. The field is strongest in two places on the magnet, called the north and south poles. On a bar-shaped magnet, the poles are at either end.

▲ A magnetic material like iron contains many tiny magnetized areas called domains. If the material is not a magnet, these domains point in different directions (a). But by rubbing another magnet on the material, the domains can be lined up, and it becomes a magnet (b).

◄ A compass needle is a small bar magnet whose north pole lines up with the Earth's magnetic field, showing us where north is.

Magnets can only attract things that also contain magnetic materials. Iron is the most common magnetic material. An iron-rich rock called magnetite, or lodestone, was one of the first natural magnets discovered. Other magnetic materials include nickel and cobalt. It is the arrangement of the electrons (the tiny particles inside atoms) in a substance that makes it magnetic or not.

Perhaps the best-known use for magnets is in compasses. Compass needles always point to the north. But why? The answer was found by William Gilbert, an English scientist, in 1600. He discovered that a compass needle is in fact a magnet, and that the Earth itself has a magnetic field, with one magnetic pole near the North Pole, and the other near the South Pole.

MICHAEL FARADAY

Michael Faraday (1791–1867) has a special place in the history of physics and engineering because his discoveries led to so many inventions. He was one of the greatest experimental scientists of all time.

Faraday invented the first electric motor, and discovered the theory of electromagnetic induction. This showed that a magnet pushed into a coil of wire generated an electric current in the coil.

Modern electric generators all use induction to make electricity. Faraday also discovered that an electric current in one wire can cause a current to flow in another wire.

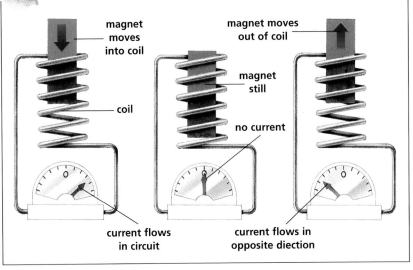

magnet moves into coil

magnet moves out of coil

coil

magnet still

no current

current flows in circuit

current flows in opposite diection

key words

- generator
- induction
- magnet
- motor

◀ Powerful electromagnets can be turned on to pick up scrap metal, then turned off to dump the metal. Similar electromagnets are used to lift and dump old cars into crushers.

Electrickery

Because magnetism depends on the behaviour of electrons, there are strong connections between electricity and magnetism. This was first noticed in 1820, by the Danish scientist Hans Christian Oersted, who saw that a current flowing through a wire made a nearby compass needle move. Later, André Ampère in France discovered that electric currents in wires can attract or repel each other, just like magnets.

Today, these principles are used to make a powerful type of magnet called an electromagnet. An electromagnet is made by passing an electric current through a coil of wire, usually wound around an iron core. When the current is switched off, the electromagnet loses its magnetism. Electromagnets are used in many electrical machines, such as generators and motors. In the home, small electromagnets work electric doorbells.

POWERING UP

cap · bicycle tyre

iron

rotating magnet

fixed coil

electric current lights bulb

What does a rock star playing an electric guitar have in common with a power station? They both use electric generators. When the musician belts out some power chords on the electric guitar, the guitar uses tiny generators to convert vibrations from the strings into electrical energy.

Generators are machines that produce (generate) electricity. They convert mechanical energy – the energy of motion – into electrical energy. The small dynamo that makes electricity for bicycle lights is a generator, driven by one of the bike's wheels. Giant spinning turbines drive the generators in power stations, which make mains electricity for our homes.

The principle behind the generator is called electromagnetic induction. It was discovered by the English scientist Michael Faraday in 1831. He found that he could produce an electrical current in a wire if he moved the wire in a certain direction near a magnet. The same happened when he moved a magnet near a wire – again, in a certain direction only. (The wires had to be

key words
- coil
- dynamo
- generator
- induction
- magnet

▼ The outer part of this generator is a large electromagnet. The hole through the centre is where the coil will go.

▲ A dynamo produces enough electricity to power the lights on a bicycle. The movement of the bicycle tyre turns the cap, which spins a magnet inside the dynamo. Around the magnet is a fixed coil. Current flows in the coil as the magnet turns.

part of a closed loop called a circuit, because you don't get a current in a wire that's not connected to anything.)

Building generators

Some generators work by moving coils of wire in a magnetic field. In some generators the coil spins on a shaft surrounded by magnets. As it spins, electricity flows through the coil. However, in a bicycle dynamo, and in the large generators used in power stations, the coil is fixed. Down the centre of it runs a shaft carrying a magnet (in a power station generator, a powerful electromagnet is used). As the magnet spins, electric current is generated in the coils.

Generators normally produce two-way, or alternating current (AC), which is why they are often called alternators. If one-way, or direct current (DC), is needed, generators must be fitted with a switching device to keep the current flowing in only one direction.

IN A SPIN

Electric motors power most of the machines we use in our homes, and most machines in industry, from drills and printing presses to trains and milk floats. In fact it probably won't be long before electric motors, using a new type of battery called a fuel cell, are powering the latest cars.

Electric motors work in the opposite way to electricity generators. They convert electricity into energy to make things move, whereas generators use movement to make electricity. The English physicist Michael Faraday made the world's first electric motor in 1822. He showed that electric current could be used to move a wire in a magnetic field.

How motors work

An electric motor is built in much the same way as a generator. It has a set of wire coils, wound round a block called an armature, and mounted on a shaft, or rotor. Magnets or electromagnets around the armature create a magnetic field.

When electric current is fed into the wires of the coils, the shaft of the motor rotates. The rotating shaft can then be used to drive machines.

Electric motors may be driven by direct (one-way) current or alternating (two-way) current. Direct current machines need a switching device called a commutator to keep the rotor spinning in the same direction.

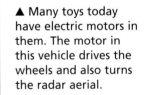

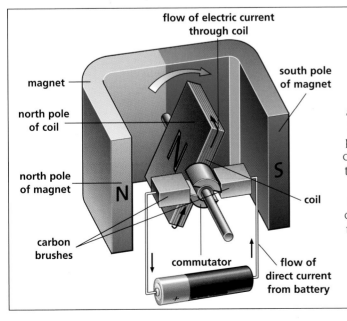

flow of electric current
through coil

magnet

north pole
of coil

south pole
of magnet

north pole
of magnet

coil

N

S

carbon
brushes

commutator

flow of
direct current
from battery

A SIMPLE MOTOR

This diagram of a simple direct-current (DC) motor shows a motor with just one turn of the wire coil. When current passes through the coil, it creates a magnetic field around the wire. This magnetic field interacts with the field between the poles of the permanent magnet. The coil turns until its own poles are next to the opposite poles of the magnet, because opposite magnetic poles attract each other. At this point, the commutator, which connects the coil to the battery, reverses the direction of the current flowing through the coil. The magnetic field around the coil is reversed, forcing the coil to make another half-turn.

▲ Many toys today have electric motors in them. The motor in this vehicle drives the wheels and also turns the radar aerial.

key words

- coil
- electromagnet
- generator
- magnet
- motor

MAKING ELECTRICITY

Switch on your TV and it flickers into life. But have you ever considered where it gets its power from? Huge, fuel-hungry power stations dotted around the country make electricity and send it to our homes through cables. One power station generates enough electricity to supply thousands of homes.

Most modern power stations make electricity by burning fuel to heat water. Heating water creates steam, which is used to turn the blades of giant turbines – just as blowing on a child's toy windmill makes it spin round. The spinning turbines drive huge machines called generators, which produce electricity.

Choice of fuels

There are several types of fuel that a power station can use to heat water. Those most

▶ White, cloud-like plumes of water vapour rise from cooling towers at a power station in Cheshire, UK.

● **key words**
- fossil fuels
- generator
- nuclear energy

often used in today's power stations are coal, gas, oil or nuclear fuel. Coal, gas and oil are known as fossil fuels, because they formed from the remains of plants and animals over millions of years.

In conventional power stations, fossil fuels are burned to heat vast quantities of water. In nuclear power stations, however, nuclear fuels such as uranium are used to make electricity. The uranium is not burnt

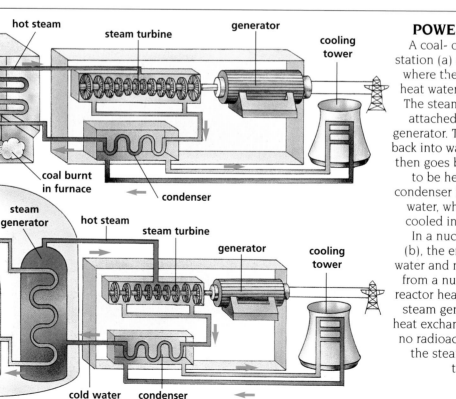

(a) coal — hot steam — steam turbine — generator — cooling tower — coal burnt in furnace — condenser

(b) nuclear reactor — steam generator — hot steam — steam turbine — generator — cooling tower — cold water — condenser

POWER STATIONS

A coal- or oil-fired power station (a) contains a furnace, where the fuel is burned to heat water and make steam. The steam drives a turbine attached to an electricity generator. The steam is turned back into water in a condenser, then goes back to the furnace to be heated again. The condenser is cooled with cold water, which is then itself cooled in a cooling tower.

In a nuclear power station (b), the energy to heat the water and make steam comes from a nuclear reactor. The reactor heats the water in the steam generator through a heat exchange system, so that no radioactivity can get into the steam powering the turbines.

in a furnace. Instead, its atoms are broken apart in a process called nuclear fission. This process creates large quantities of heat, which is used to produce high-pressure steam.

Burning fossil fuels in power stations creates pollution that causes damage to the Earth's atmosphere. It may cause acid rain, for example. Nuclear power stations cause no air pollution, but they produce wastes that are radioactive (give off dangerous radiation).

Alternative energy

Because using fuel to make electricity damages the environment, scientists have found different (alternative) ways of generating electricity. Hydroelectric power stations are one way of doing this. They use the power of the water that cascades down a waterfall or a dam, to turn a turbine – without making harmful waste materials.

▼ A model of what was probably the world's first power station, built by Thomas Edison (1847–1931). Edison invented light bulbs in 1879, and realized that many people would want electric light in their homes. He decided that he would have to set up power stations to provide electricity for them. So he designed the first power station at Pearl Street in New York. The station was 'switched on' in 1882.

▲ Some people think they are an eyesore, but wind farms provide energy without damaging the environment.

Wind is also a harmless source of power. Armies of giant windmills – called wind farms – are springing up both on land and at sea. The propellers of the windmills spin round and turn generators when the wind blows. The electricity the windmills generate can also charge batteries, which then supply power when the wind drops.

Power from the sun is another great hope for the future. At present solar power is expensive, but scientists are trying to find ways of producing it more cheaply. Geothermal energy is also being examined. This involves using the tremendous heat trapped in the Earth's crust – perhaps 15 kilometres below ground – to heat water and drive turbines.

SUPPLY ON DEMAND

Stretching all over the country, thousands and thousands of kilometres of cables carry electricity to factories, offices and homes. These cables are carried by tall pylons (towers) or buried underground. They join many power stations in a vast network, called a national grid.

Power stations produce electricity at a voltage (electrical pressure) of about 20,000 volts. It is alternating current (AC), which means that the current changes direction many times per second.

But it is not economic to transmit (send) electricity over long distances at 20,000 volts. Too much power would be lost. If the electricity is transmitted at a much higher voltage, the power losses are much lower.

All change!

The kind of electricity produced by power stations is called alternating current (AC). AC does not travel through the cables in one direction only, but changes direction many times a second. It is easy to change the voltage of AC electricity, using a device called a transformer. At the power station a 'step-up' transformer boosts the generated voltage to as much as 500,000 volts. The power travels along high-voltage cables (which lose much less power) to where it is needed.

▶ A simple transformer. A voltage applied to the primary coil produces a voltage in the secondary coil. If the secondary coil is smaller than the primary coil, the transformer reduces the voltage (step-down). If the secondary coil is bigger, the voltage is stepped up.

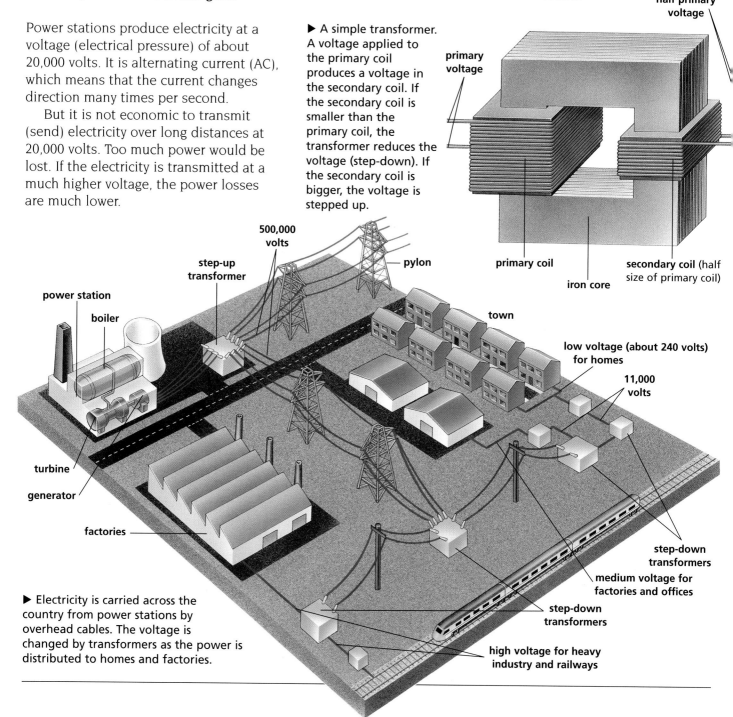

half primary voltage

primary voltage

primary coil

iron core

secondary coil (half size of primary coil)

500,000 volts

step-up transformer

pylon

power station

boiler

town

low voltage (about 240 volts) for homes

11,000 volts

turbine

generator

factories

step-down transformers

medium voltage for factories and offices

step-down transformers

high voltage for heavy industry and railways

▶ Electricity is carried across the country from power stations by overhead cables. The voltage is changed by transformers as the power is distributed to homes and factories.

Of course, we don't want electricity coming into our homes at 500,000 volts! Other transformers are used to 'step down' the voltage to more useful levels: several thousand volts for factories, and about 240 volts for homes. This process normally happens at local substations.

Electricity in the home

We call the electricity that comes into our homes 'mains electricity'. It travels to where it is needed along circuits. There are separate circuits for different things. One may carry heavy current to drive an electric cooker. Another will power the sockets we use to plug in things like dishwashers and TVs. A third circuit powers the lights.

Occasionally a broken machine might use more electricity than is safe, and could catch fire. To prevent this, plugs are fitted with fuses. These are thin pieces of wire that melt when too much current flows through them, so breaking the circuit.

A circuit-breaker is another safety device that we have in our homes. This cuts off the electricity automatically if the amount of current flowing in a circuit gets too high.

▼ The pylon in the background (left) brings high-voltage electricity to the transformers (centre) in this electricity substation.

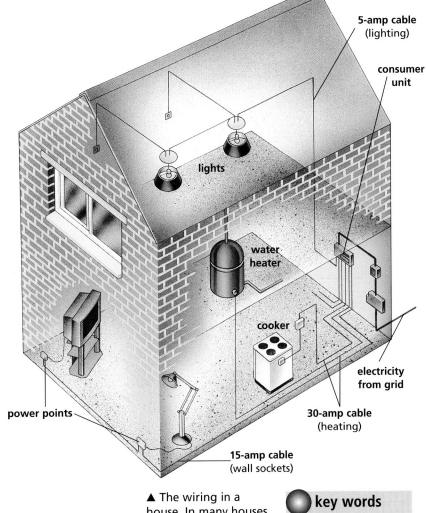

5-amp cable (lighting)

consumer unit

lights

water heater

cooker

electricity from grid

power points

30-amp cable (heating)

15-amp cable (wall sockets)

▲ The wiring in a house. In many houses, the main cable branches out to several circuits at the consumer unit. The power points are usually all connected to the same cable, called a ring main.

key words
- voltage
- power station
- alternating current
- transformer
- fuse

Powerful plug-ins

Companies that supply electricity keep a constant check on how much electricity people are using. Sometimes, more electricity is being used in an area than is available. The electricity company will then connect to other power stations in the grid and use some of their electricity.

Electricity supply is now a big international business. This means that different countries can share electricity if they have some to spare. At peak times, for instance, when everybody is using electricity, Britain can use power from France.

INCREDIBLE SHRINKING CIRCUITS

a single transistor

Mobile phones, pocket computers and many other devices have been made possible by the incredible advances in electronics since the mid-20th century. Of all the devices invented since then, none has matched the impact of the transistor.

The transistor is at the heart of electronics. This is the branch of electrical engineering involving small-scale devices. Where electrical engineers tend to look at heavy currents in large devices, electronics engineers are concerned with light currents in small devices.

aluminium (for electrical connections

layers of treated silicon form circuit components

silicon wafer

whole microchip

electronic circuits

More from less

One of the most important jobs an electronic circuit does is to make a small signal into a bigger one. This is called

microchip

plastic base

connector pins

microchip on base

THE FIRST TRANSISTOR

In 1947, three scientists working at the Bell Telephone Laboratories in New Jersey, USA, made an important breakthrough in electronics. John Bardeen (1908–1991), Walter Brattain (1902–1987) and William Shockley (1910–1989) used a semiconductor called germanium to make the world's first transistor. The three scientists shared the Nobel Prize for Physics in 1956.

The invention of the transistor, shown below resting on a fingertip, made it possible to build much smaller and more reliable electronic circuits.

▼ A transistor on a fingertip.

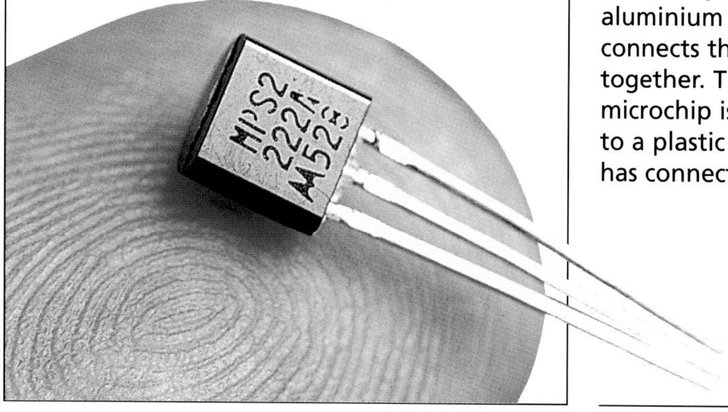

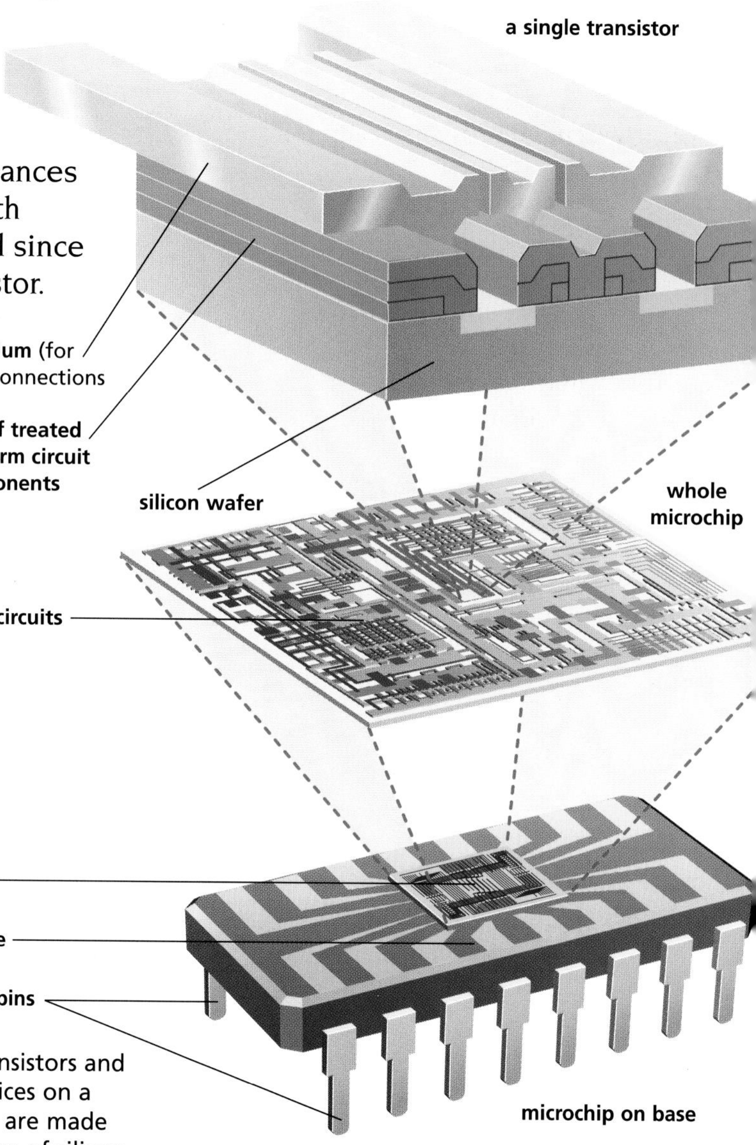

▲ The transistors and other devices on a microchip are made up of layers of silicon, treated in different ways to have different electrical properties. A final layer of aluminium 'tracks' connects the devices together. The complete microchip is fastened to a plastic base, which has connector pins.

amplification. When you turn up the volume on your hi-fi, you are amplifying the electrical signal that produces the sound.

Early amplifiers used big, fragile devices called valves to amplify signals. The development of the transistor, a small 'sandwich' made of semiconducting material, was an important step in electronics. Transistors provided amplification from a very low-powered device the size of a peanut.

The first transistor radios appeared in 1955. Soon transistors were being used in all sorts of gadgets, such as TVs and hi-fis. Transistors also helped to make equipment in spacecraft much lighter.

In the 1970s integrated circuits (microchips), containing many transistors and other parts on one tiny chip of silicon, began to replace individual transistors. Now there are millions of transistors in the microchip circuits used in computers.

Capacitors and diodes

Capacitors and diodes are two other devices used in electronic circuits.

A diode conducts electricity easily in one direction, but resists the flow of electricity in the other. It is an important part of many circuits.

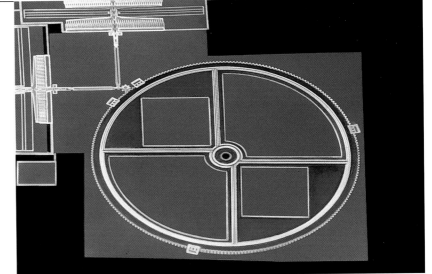

A capacitor stores electric charge between two conducting plates. It takes a certain amount of time for a capacitor to charge up. So capacitors are important components for making timers.

Capacitors can also be used in filtering circuits. These get rid of signals you don't want. When you turn up the bass and turn down the treble on your hi-fi, you are using filtering circuits.

▲ Future electronic devices may include minute motors like this one, etched on to a wafer of silicon. Two 'microengines' at top left (green and yellow) turn a tiny gear (centre), which is smaller in diameter than a human hair.

television

radio

digital music player

▲ Radios, TVs, personal stereos and many other devices we use every day rely on electronics to work.

LOGIC GATES

As well as working as amplifiers, transistors can be used to switch signals on and off. This makes them particularly useful for circuits called logic gates, which are central to computers. An OR logic gate, for example (a), has two inputs. An electrical pulse can pass through the 'gate' if there is a signal from either or both inputs. A NOT gate (b) lets a pulse through if there is no input, but doesn't let it through if there is an input. These and other logic gates can be combined to make circuits that can work out simple sums. A computer's central processor has thousands of such circuits.

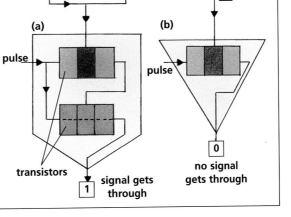

key words
- amplifier
- capacitor
- diode
- filtering
- logic gate
- transistor

GETTING THE MESSAGE

'That's one small step for a man, one giant leap for mankind', said the US astronaut Neil Armstrong in 1969, as he took his first steps on the Moon. Radio signals beamed Armstrong's words and TV pictures live to Earth, and they were broadcast around the world.

The Moon landing broadcasts were a triumph of modern communications. But today, people can communicate in many more ways than in 1969, using mobile phones, faxes, emails and satellite links.

▶ A sound or a picture can be recorded as an analogue signal – an electrical copy of the sound or image. This signal changes smoothly. But modern communications are mostly digital. In a digital signal, the sound or picture is 'sampled' (measured) at regular intervals. The string of measurements is the digital signal.

Reaching out

However different they are, all communication systems have one thing in common. They turn a message – made up of spoken words, music, text or pictures – into something that can be sent (transmitted) in some way. This is called a 'signal'. At the receiving end, the signal is turned back into the message.

One of the first long-distance communication systems, invented in 1790, was the semaphore tower. Semaphore

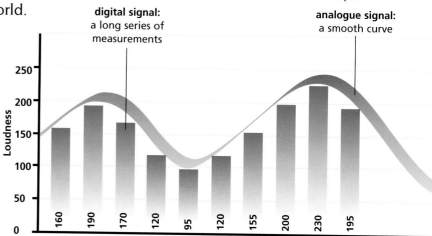

digital signal: a long series of measurements

analogue signal: a smooth curve

Loudness: 250, 200, 150, 100, 50, 0

160 190 170 120 95 120 155 200 230 195

towers had two long wooden arms that could be moved to different positions. Each position of the arms stood for a different letter or number. Using semaphore, messages could be sent between distant hilltops many kilometres apart. But semaphore was very slow.

Going electric

Communications speeded up after the discovery in 1821 that an electric current flowing in a wire can make a compass needle turn. This led to the invention of the telegraph, which could send messages both further and faster than semaphore.

◀ Digital phone calls can be transmitted as flashes of light, through cables made of optical fibre. Today, most telephone networks use fibre, as they can carry more calls.

▶ A type of semaphore signalling was used by sailors for many years to communicate between ships. The sailors signalled using two flags, one in either hand.

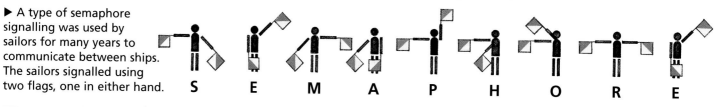

S E M A P H O R E

Telegraphs sent different electric currents down the wires. At the receiver, these made needles point to different letters or numbers.

The telegraph became faster with the invention of a springy switch called a telegraph key, which could send messages in Morse code. This coded letters and numbers as mixtures of short 'dots' or longer 'dashes' of electric current.

Sounds and waves

The invention of the telephone in 1876 made it possible for people to actually speak to each other, rather than sending messages by code. As with the telegraph, the messages were sent as electrical signals along wires.

Radio waves can also carry communications. Television, radio, telephone and Internet signals can all be sent this way. Radio waves travel in straight lines. This means that over long distances radio signals do not follow the curved surface of the

▼ Some mobile phone masts are made to look like trees so that they blend into the environment.

Earth. Satellites circling in space can be used to send such signals around the world. The satellite receives a signal – such as a TV sports broadcast – then re-transmits it to another part of the Earth that could not be reached otherwise.

Calls on the move

Mobile phones transmit messages using radio-type waves called microwaves. Special masts with aerials that can send and receive mobile phone transmissions are dotted all over the country. A call from a mobile usually goes to the nearest of these masts. If the receiving phone is a mobile too, the signals travel through the telephone network to the mast nearest to the receiving phone. This mast then transmits the call via microwaves.

Modern mobiles and television networks send very clear digital signals. These turn a normal, or analogue signal, into a stream of numbers.

SAMUEL MORSE'S CODE

The US inventor Samuel Morse (1791–1872) became interested in the telegraph in the 1830s. He eventually developed the system of dots and dashes that became known as Morse code. He demonstrated the code for the first time in 1844.

Although Morse code was punched into paper tape at the telegraph receiver, operators found they could decode it much quicker by simply listening to the noise made by the tape punch.

▶ The alphabet and numbers 1 to 10 in Morse code.

A ●▬	B ▬●●●	C ▬●▬●	D ▬●●
E ●	F ●●▬●	G ▬▬●	H ●●●●
I ●●	J ●▬▬▬	K ▬●▬	L ●▬●●
M ▬▬	N ▬●	O ▬▬▬	P ●▬▬●
Q ▬▬●▬	R ●▬●	S ●●●	T ▬
U ●●▬	V ●●●▬	W ●▬▬	X ▬●●▬
Y ▬●▬▬	Z ▬▬●●	1 ●▬▬▬▬	2 ●●▬▬▬
3 ●●●▬▬	4 ●●●●▬	5 ●●●●●	6 ▬●●●●
7 ▬▬●●●	8 ▬▬▬●●	9 ▬▬▬▬●	10 ▬▬▬▬▬

key words

- telegraph
- semaphore
- message
- transmission
- digital
- analogue

PUTTING YOU THROUGH

Mobile phones have given people the freedom to make calls from just about anywhere. As a result, they have helped save many lives. Stranded mountaineers, people on sinking boats – even hot-air balloonists in trouble – have all used mobiles to call for help.

Mobiles are a very recent invention. But telephones were invented more than a hundred years ago. Telephones have changed a great deal since the early days, but the way the telephone system works is still basically the same. So just what happens when you make a phone call?

Current voices

When you punch in a phone number, the telephone sends the number to a place called an 'exchange'. The exchange connects you up to the person you want to contact.

When the person you are ringing picks up the phone, you speak into the handset. A microphone in your handset changes

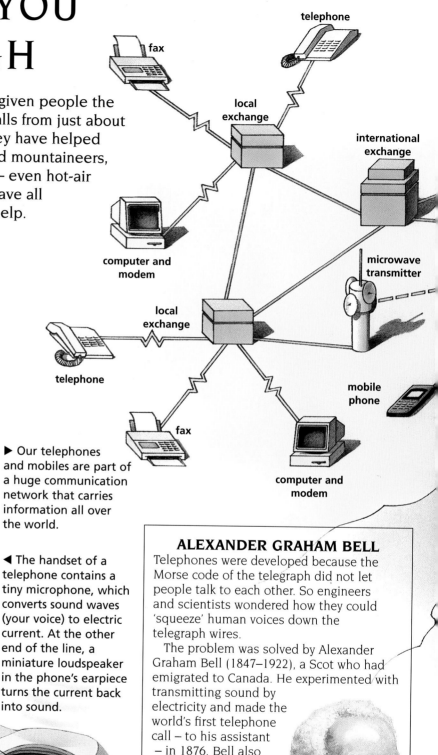

▶ Our telephones and mobiles are part of a huge communication network that carries information all over the world.

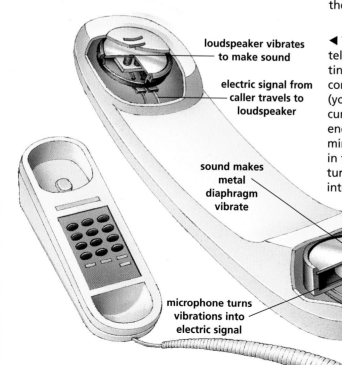

loudspeaker vibrates to make sound

electric signal from caller travels to loudspeaker

sound makes metal diaphragm vibrate

microphone turns vibrations into electric signal

◀ The handset of a telephone contains a tiny microphone, which converts sound waves (your voice) to electric current. At the other end of the line, a miniature loudspeaker in the phone's earpiece turns the current back into sound.

ALEXANDER GRAHAM BELL

Telephones were developed because the Morse code of the telegraph did not let people talk to each other. So engineers and scientists wondered how they could 'squeeze' human voices down the telegraph wires.

The problem was solved by Alexander Graham Bell (1847–1922), a Scot who had emigrated to Canada. He experimented with transmitting sound by electricity and made the world's first telephone call – to his assistant – in 1876. Bell also invented the telephone exchange. The first exchange, with just 20 lines, was installed in Connecticut, USA, in 1877. Britain's first exchange opened in 1879.

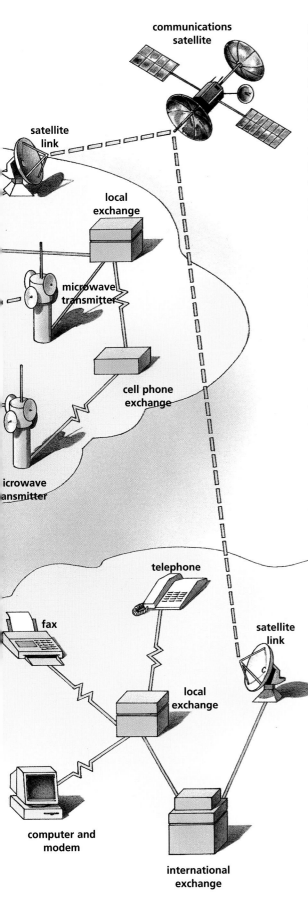

communications
satellite

satellite
link

local
exchange

microwave
transmitter

cell phone
exchange

icrowave
ansmitter

telephone

fax

satellite
link

local
exchange

computer and
modem

international
exchange

sound waves from your voice into an electric signal. This signal is then sent through the telephone system to the other phone. At the receiving end, the electrical signal drives a tiny loudspeaker in the handset, which reproduces your voice.

But why are telephone exchanges necessary? It's because if every phone in the world was connected to every other, we would be awash in wires. Instead, each phone is connected to a local exchange, which connects in turn to other exchanges.

Early exchanges used operators who plugged your line into the one of the person you were calling. But that was only possible when there were few telephone users. As phones became more popular, automatic exchanges were introduced.

Light fantastic

In modern phone networks, the sound of your voice is not only sent down electrical wires – it is transmitted in many other ways. Many telephone cables are now made up of optical fibres, which can carry more calls than wires. Instead of transmitting the sound of your voice as electrical signals, optical fibres carry the voice information as tiny pulses of light.

Phone networks also use radio waves and microwaves to send information from place to place. Radio links, called relays, are used particularly in places where it's hard to put up telegraph poles. Satellite links, and undersea optical fibre cables, are used to connect phones across the oceans. Telephone networks are also used to transmit information over the internet and to send faxes.

Phones of the future

Modern mobile phones can do much more than just make calls. They can send faxes and emails, store phone numbers and other information, and connect up with your computer and, to a limited extent, the internet.

Soon videophones will let people see each other using built-in cameras and small video screens. You will also be able to use them to watch other kinds of videos, and to surf the Internet.

key words
- loudspeaker
- microphone
- mobile phone
- telephone exchange

▲ A videophone allows two people to have a conversation and see each other at the same time.

DIGITAL TRANSMITTERS

Did you know that you can squeeze pictures down your telephone line? A fax machine lets you do just that. And phone lines can carry other information besides voices and pictures.

Phone lines are useful for sending documents to people by fax. But if you have a modem and internet connection, you can also use a phone line for surfing the web and keeping in touch by email.

Fax is short for facsimile, which means 'identical copy'. Fax machines turn an image or document into information that can be sent down a phone line. Modems can also send information down a phone line – in this case, computer data. A computer with a modem can send faxes, too.

Sending and getting faxes

Once a fax machine gets through to the machine it is sending to, light sensors inside it scan across the page in a series of

▶ Sending and receiving a simple image via a fax. Telephone lines were designed originally only to carry voice signals, and this means that the speed at which a fax can work is limited.

key words
- document
- fax
- modem

light sensors

sending fax

Light sensors change blacks and whites of image into electrical 0s and 1s.

thin lines. Scanning turns the pattern of light and dark on each line of the original into electrical signals, which are sent through the telephone system to the receiving fax machine. This machine takes the signals one line at a time. It sends them to a line of tiny heating elements. Where the original document was dark, the heating element is turned on. Where it was light, the element is turned off. Heat-sensitive paper moves past the heating elements, and where the elements are on, the paper turns black. Gradually, the pattern of light and dark on the original document is drawn at the receiving fax.

◀ Missed the post? Birthday wishes are just one kind of message that can be sent anywhere in the world over the Internet. The picture and text are stored on computer as digital information. A modem converts this information into packets of electrical signals that can be sent down the phone line.

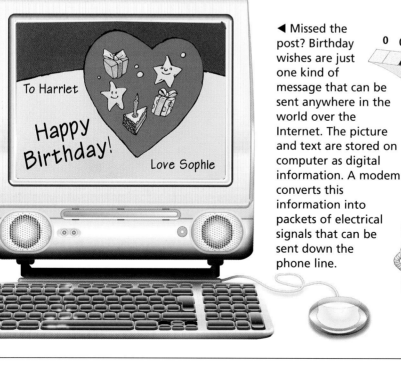

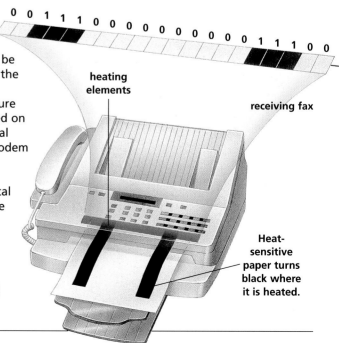

heating elements

receiving fax

Heat-sensitive paper turns black where it is heated.

WIRELESS WONDER

It is 12 December 1901. In St John's, Newfoundland, on the east coast of Canada, a team of people are struggling to raise a long aerial into the stormy skies. Supported by balloons and kites, the aerial is at last raised. Miraculously, it picks up faint signals – the letter S in Morse code. The signal comes from Poldhu in Cornwall, England. It is the first international radio broadcast.

The driving force behind the first transatlantic radio transmission was the Italian inventor Guglielmo Marconi. He had been experimenting with sending radio, or 'wireless', messages for six years. In December 1901 he proved that radio could be a new way for the whole world to communicate.

Today, radio stations in every country broadcast programmes to billions of people. And two-way radio links connect mobile phones, aircraft with airports, ships with the shore, and spacecraft with Earth.

key words

- broadcast
- radio waves
- sound signal
- transmitter
- wireless

▲ Clockwork radios work without an electricity supply or batteries. The clockwork spring turns a generator, which makes electricity.

recorded. This is called a sound signal. The sound signal is combined with a more powerful signal called the carrier wave. The combined signal goes to a transmitter, a metal antenna on a tall mast that sends out the signal as radio waves. The radio waves travel through the air to your radio receiver, where an electrical circuit, called a demodulator, extracts the original sound.

How radio works

In a radio studio, microphones make an electrical 'copy' of the sound being

▼ How a radio broadcast reaches your radio at home.

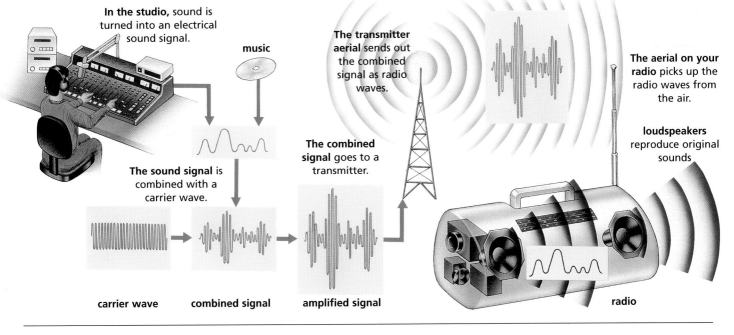

In the studio, sound is turned into an electrical sound signal.

music

The transmitter aerial sends out the combined signal as radio waves.

The aerial on your radio picks up the radio waves from the air.

loudspeakers reproduce original sounds

The sound signal is combined with a carrier wave.

The combined signal goes to a transmitter.

carrier wave   combined signal   amplified signal   radio

PICTURE PERFECT

When we watch television, we can cheer our favourite sports teams from our living-rooms, or hear news of earthquakes and wars on the other side of the world. We can watch movies, soaps and music videos, too. Satellite, cable and digital TV have added hundreds of extra TV channels. Soon, interactive TV will let us take part in programmes from home.

camera   **filters separate light into red, blue and green parts**   **viewfinder**

lens system

colour detectors   **signals from detectors split into colour and brightness parts**

▲ A TV camera captures a moving scene and sends a TV signal to your home via a transmitting aerial or an optical cable.

But have you ever wondered just how those pictures and sounds get on to your TV set? Television is a system that sends and receives pictures and sounds. A television camera records the pictures; a microphone records the sounds. The camera changes the images from light rays into electrical signals. These are sent to your TV set (television receiver). The receiver changes the electrical signals back to light again.

On camera

To make a TV picture, the camera focuses the scene being filmed onto three light-sensitive microchips called charge-coupled devices (CCDs). Each CCD is sensitive to a different type of light: one to red light, one to green and one to blue.

Each CCD has millions of tiny 'wells' sunk into its surface. When light falls on the CCD, each well becomes electrically charged, with a charge equal to the brightness of the light at that point. Together, the three CCDs produce an electric 'picture' of the brightness of red, blue and green light throughout the scene.

A TV camera does not capture a moving scene as whole pictures. Instead, it scans across the scene in a series of lines. The camera scans a complete set of lines 25 times each second.

Sending the pictures

To get the action to your home, the electric 'pictures' from the camera and the sound information from the microphone are collected together into a TV signal. The signal is combined with a carrier wave, a powerful electric current that can be used to create radio waves.

The carrier wave, carrying its TV signal, can be used to send out radio waves from a transmitting aerial on a high TV mast. Your TV aerial then picks up these radio waves. The signal may also travel to your home as flashes of light along an optical cable. Satellite TV programs are beamed up to a communications satellite in orbit around Earth. The satellite then sends a signal back to Earth, which is picked up by your satellite dish.

BAIRD'S BOX

John Logie Baird (1888–1946), a Scot, was the first person to make a moving television picture. He used a mechanical way of scanning each line of his TV picture, using a spinning perforated disc invented by a Greman scientist, Paul Nipkow. In the UK, the BBC set up the world's first public TV broadcasting company using Baird's device, but it was soon replaced by a better, electronic system.

key words
- CCD
- CRT
- electron beam
- radio waves
- scanning
- transmission

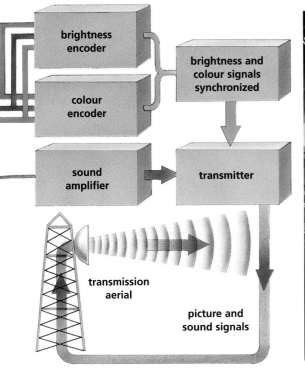

On screen

Most TVs still use a glass cathode-ray tube (CRT) to display pictures. At the narrow end of a CRT are three electron 'guns'. Each fires a beam of electrons at the TV screen, which is coated with a material called phosphor. Where the beam hits the screen, the phosphor glows. The three electron guns light up red, green and blue phosphor dots on the screen.

▲ A television programme being filmed in front of a studio audience. Using lighting, sets and special effects it is possible to create all kinds of different scenes in a TV studio.

The TV signal controls the red, blue and green electron guns. As the beams scan across the screen, the TV signal changes the strength of each beam, recreating the pattern of light and darkness in the original picture. Although the picture is only in three colours, different mixtures of the three cause our eyes to see other colours as well.

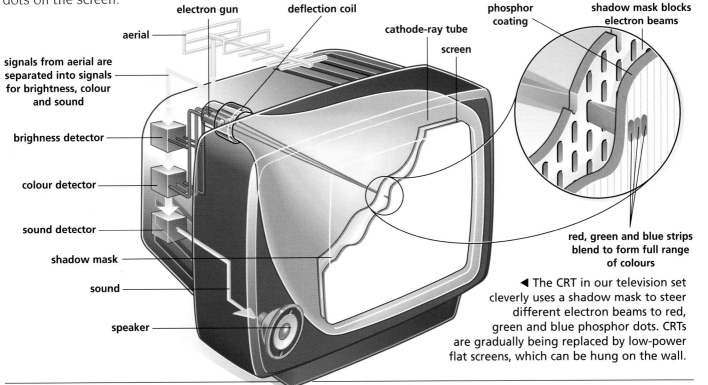

red, green and blue strips blend to form full range of colours

◀ The CRT in our television set cleverly uses a shadow mask to steer different electron beams to red, green and blue phosphor dots. CRTs are gradually being replaced by low-power flat screens, which can be hung on the wall.

TV ON VIDEO

H ome videotaping means you don't have to rush home to watch your favourite TV programmes. By simply setting a timer, you can watch what you want, anytime. And portable cameras, with video recorders built in, let you make your own home movies. But how does videotape work?

TV pictures can be recorded on magnetic tape in the same way that sound is recorded on a tape recorder. The main machine used is called a video cassette recorder (VCR), in which the tape is normally on a cassette. But TV pictures contain too much information to fit on an ordinary audio tape. The tape would have to run so fast that it would snap.

▶ Just the batteries of an early video camera were bigger than this tiny palmcorder. Miniature microchips and tiny mechanical parts make today's video cameras unbelievably small.

◀ Editing TV programmes has been made easier by computers.

🔵 key words
- helical scanning
- recording
- VCR

Digital rivals

Traditional video tapes are being replaced by machines such as DVD players, which record videos digitally. These store the information about the pictures and sound in the same way that a computer stores information on its hard disk.

With digital video recordings it is easy to edit TV programmes or home movies. You can record digital pictures on to computers, then cut and paste the footage where you want it, just like the text in a word processor!

▼ Inside a video recorder, the tape runs over the spinning video head drum and past the audio (sound) head. The sound track is recorded along the top of the tape. The video head records the pictures as diagonal tracks across the tape, resting side by side like fallen dominoes.

Tilted drums

The answer to this problem is to use wider tape, and tape heads (the part that 'reads' the tape) that spin rapidly rather the stationary ones used for sound recording.

The heads in a video machine are on opposite sides of a circular drum that is tilted slightly in relation to the direction that the tape moves in. During recording or playback, the tape wraps around the drum. As the drum spins very fast, it 'wipes' thin diagonal stripes of the TV signal on to the slowly moving tape. This is called helical scanning.

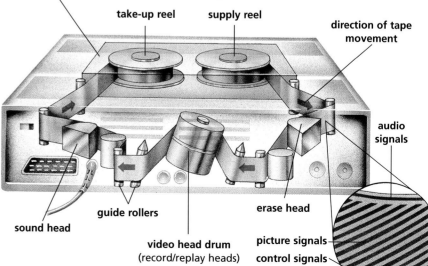

video cassette

take-up reel   supply reel

direction of tape movement

audio signals

guide rollers

sound head

erase head

video head drum (record/replay heads)

picture signals

control signals

BILLIONS OF BYTES

Thud! You feel the wheels of your aircraft touch down on the runway – but you're surprised that you've landed already. Outside, the fog's so thick you thought you were still up in the clouds. So how did the pilots manage to land the aircraft without seeing the runway? Well, they had a computer to help them.

Computers are very good at storing and handling information (data). The Internet provides a vast store of data that we can all tap into from a computer at home.

Computers are also very good at controlling all kinds of machines, from dishwashers to the space shuttle. In industry, computers are at the heart of control systems that run everything from car assembly lines to oil refineries.

How computers work

But what exactly is a computer? It is an electronic machine that works under the control of a list of instructions called a program. The computer takes in data, which is called an input. It processes the data in a central processing unit (CPU). The CPU contains one or more microchips, or microprocessors. A microprocessor is basically a calculator that performs a few simple types of sums very quickly.

The result of all the processing is called the computer's output. The computer is called the hardware, while the program is the software.

Only two numbers

Most computers are digital computers. This means they handle all their data in the form of binary numbers. The two numbers in binary are simply 0 and 1 (the decimal system we count in runs from 0 to 9). Binary is easy for a computer to deal with. The

▲ Tiny notebook computers like this one can link to the Internet over mobile phone networks.

▼ In older aircraft, the pilot controlled the plane using mechanical links from the cockpit controls to the plane's engine, flaps and rudder. But in airliners like this Airbus A340, computers can control the aircraft by sending electrical signals to the engine, flaps and rudder.

microprocessor contains millions of tiny electronic switches equivalent to miniature transistors, which can be turned on or off. 'On' can represent the 1 in a binary number, and 'Off' can represent the 0. Using these simple numbers, the microprocessor is able to do sums at lightning speed.

It's not just calculations that a computer uses binary numbers for. Words, pictures and sounds are all created, changed and stored digitally using binary numbers. In a word processing program each letter and number is coded for by a particular binary number. Pictures are broken up into tiny dots (pixels), and the brightness and colour of each pixel is coded as a binary number. Sounds can also be coded for in a similar way.

Total recall

The computer's software is stored in a memory of some kind. A computer has two kinds of memory, stored on microchips. The software that controls how the

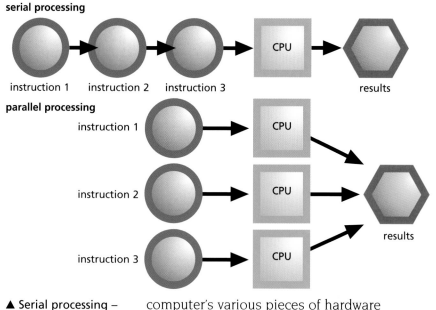

serial processing

instruction 1   instruction 2   instruction 3   CPU   results

parallel processing

instruction 1 — CPU
instruction 2 — CPU — results
instruction 3 — CPU

▲ Serial processing – working on one piece of data at a time – is slow but cheap, while parallel processing is fast but expensive.

▼ A timeline of some of the important events in the history of computing.

computer's various pieces of hardware operate is stored in a memory that cannot be interfered with. This is called the Read-Only Memory, or ROM.

Before the computer starts up a program, the software will be sitting on a disk. When the computer software is running, this software will be copied into another memory, where it can be used much faster than from a disk. This memory is called the Random Access Memory, or RAM.

In operation

The operating system (OS) is a piece of software that controls how the user works the computer. Some systems use a lot of

1830s
British mathematician Charles Babbage (1791–1871) designs a machine to calculate numbers correctly. Although it was not built, his Difference Engine contained ideas used in computers today.

1890s
American Hermann Hollerith (1860–1929) develops a machine that uses punched cards to calculate the results of the 1890 US census. In 1896 Hollerith sets up the company that later becomes IBM.

1940s
The ideas of British mathematician Alan Turing (1912–1954) lead to the development of computers like the Colossus, which helps crack German secret codes in World War II.

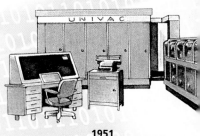

1951
Univac-1 (above), the world's first commercial computer, is designed by John Mauchly (1907–1980) and J. Presper Eckert (1919–1995). Mauchly and Eckert built ENIAC, the first electronic computer, in 1946.

'windows' and small pictures called icons, which represent different programs. You point to them, then click using a hand-held device called a mouse. Other operating systems, like those in early PCs, have a rather boring screen in which you enter commands, such as 'run word processor,' using a keyboard.

Call an architect

The way computers process data can be chosen to best match the task in hand. In a serial processor, a microprocessor carries out the first part of the task it has to do, then the next part, then the next, and so on. In a parallel processor, software divides up a task and splits it between many microprocessors, which all work on it at the same time.

Parallel processing is very fast, but also very expensive. Some parallel processors are so fast that they are called supercomputers.

Supercomputers are used for very special projects like weather forecasting or making computer models of the surface of the Sun. They might be used to predict hurricanes – which could save lives, if they help raise the alarm in time. Supercomputers are needed for such jobs because so many

▲ Computers can be built into many gadgets. This electronic 'pen' can scan text into its memory and then translate it into many different languages.

things happen at once in weather systems that only a very powerful computer can hope to keep track of them.

Future ideas

The microchips in today's computers are made up of thousands of tiny transistors, made from silicon. But future machines could use even smaller parts, capable of even greater speeds. Some scientists want to use single chemical molecules (groups of atoms) as computer on/off switches. Meanwhile, others think that single atoms, or even parts of atoms, could be used to make 'quantum' computers.

key words
- binary numbers
- hardware
- microprocessor
- program
- software

1968
'Mainframe' computers beginning to be used in large businesses.

1976
The first supercomputer, the Cray-1, is built. Modern supercomputers are used for weather forecasting, complex maths and physics problems, and animation in modern films.

1981
IBM produce the IBM PC, with software written by American Bill Gates (born 1955). The machine is a success for IBM, and for Gates's company Microsoft.

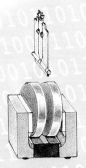

1998
A team of researchers at IBM build a very simple quantum computer. Quantum computers work using single atoms or even electrons. They have the potential to be enormously more powerful than ordinary computers.

MICROCHIP MAGIC

Computers might be powerful, but the bits that do all the hard work are tiny. The 'brains' of a computer are made of microchips, each one a flat sliver of silicon smaller than a fingernail. Microchips can contain millions of unbelievably small electronic parts.

But it's not just computers that use microchips. You'll find them in almost every electronic gadget you can think of. In a car, they may help control the braking system. They could even be in your toaster, controlling how brown the toast gets. But what has made microchips so popular?

Cool, cheap, light and fast

The electronic circuits that were used before microchips were invented used lots of separate parts all wired together. These included transistors, which switch signals on and off, resistors, which oppose currents, and diodes, which let current go one way only.

But in large electronic circuits the wiring gets hot and can burn out. And all those separate parts are quite big – a

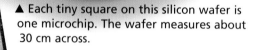

▲ Each tiny square on this silicon wafer is one microchip. The wafer measures about 30 cm across.

▲ This magnified photo of a single microchip shows how all the parts have been packed into the smallest possible space, so that none of the expensive silicon is wasted.

transistor is about the size of a jelly bean – so conventional circuits need a lot of space.

Microchips overcome these problems by using laser light and special chemicals to 'grow' tiny circuits on a thin wafer of very pure silicon. The special chemicals, called dopants, are used to alter the electrical properties of the silicon in different ways, making tiny areas that behave like transistors, or resistors, or diodes. No wires are needed – the different parts can be grown side by side. The result is a tiny circuit that stays cool. And because all the parts are so close, the chip works very fast.

key words
- dopant
- silicon
- transistor

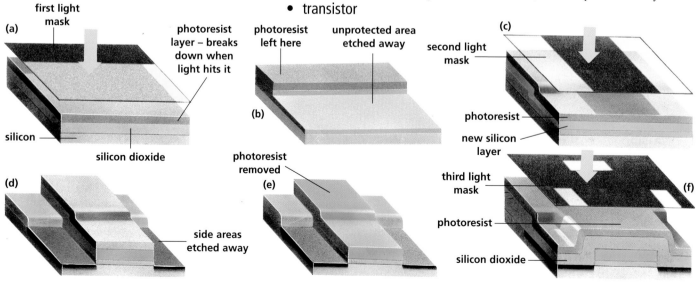

(a) first light mask
photoresist layer – breaks down when light hits it
silicon
silicon dioxide

(b) photoresist left here
unprotected area etched away

(c) second light mask
photoresist
new silicon layer

(d) side areas etched away

(e) photoresist removed

(f) third light mask
photoresist
silicon dioxide

A chip off the block

To make a chip, the circuit first has to be designed. Engineers have to design chips using computer design software because there are simply too many components to draw by hand. The first microprocessor chip had 2300 transistors, but today's chips can have more than 30 million!

Once it has been told what the microchip should do, the designer's computer works out which components are needed and how they should connect up.

Laser stencils

The microchip is made in several layers, so when the design is correct, a picture of each layer is printed onto a series of glass 'masks'. These masks are used like stencils. The first mask is placed over the silicon wafer, then a laser is shone through it.

The wafer is coated with a tough coating that is sensitive to light. The areas where the laser hits the coating are changed, and can be washed away with an acid. Dopant chemicals are then injected into the chip. Where the coating has been washed away the dopant can reach the silicon below. In this way, the different dopants can be placed on exactly the right areas to form the electronic circuit.

Making contacts

Components in the chip are connected together by metal tracks laid down after the circuit parts have been made on top

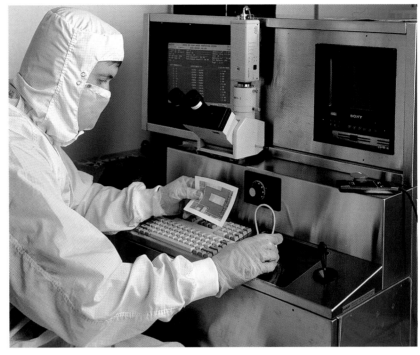

▲ The slightest impurity can ruin a microchip, so the people who make them and test them have to wear special suits and masks, and work in dust-free 'clean rooms'. The chips are made in a vacuum, so that the dopants do not become contaminated by impurities in the air.

of the chip. There can be many layers of these connectors, separated by glass 'insulator' layers.

When the chip is finished, it is sawn off the wafer and placed in a plastic package. Thin wires are stretched from the chip to contacts that stick out of the package. The chip is then tested – if it works, it is ready to be soldered onto a circuit board.

aluminium electrical contacts

finished transister

(g)

◄ The complicated sequence of adding and etching away layers involved in making a single transistor on a microchip.

THE FIRST MICROCHIPS

The American Jack Kilby (born 1923), working for the company Texas Instruments, was the first to develop an integrated circuit. In 1964 he worked out how to make more than one transistor in a sliver of a material called germanium. By 'growing' the transistors together at the same time, he found he could connect them together internally without wires. In 2000 Jack Kilby was awarded the Nobel Prize for Physics, for his part in developing integrated circuits.

Around the same time another American, Robert Noyce (1927–1990), working for Fairchild Semiconductors, made a similar microchip from silicon. Silicon ultimately became the standard microchip-making material.

HARD-WIRED

magnetic heads read disks

The computer's hard disk drive is actually a number of disks, one on top of the other. Each one has its own recording and playback head. Using a number of disks makes storing and retrieving data much faster.

O ne day, scientists will be able to make plastic computers that can be rolled up and put in your pocket. These computers will have colour screens made of an amazing bendy plastic that makes light when electric current passes through it.

hard disk drive stack

Plastic computers and screens are still some way off. In the meantime, we must make do with rigid screens.

The computer and screen are part of what is called computer hardware. This contrasts with the software – the programs and instructions that run the computer.

The main computer unit is the box that contains all the electronic circuits that make the computer work, such as the processing and memory units. These are circuit boards carrying microchips and other parts. The main computer unit also has sockets to plug in to other hardware, and a power supply. It also contains one or more disk drives.

processing unit

Window on a computer's world

The screen (called a monitor or VDU) helps us keep a check on how the computer is working, and displays information and pictures.

The common type of monitor uses a cathode-ray tube (CRT). These tubes are big and take up a lot of desk space.

Some newer computers have flat-screen monitors. They use only a third of the power of a CRT and take up much less space. But they are more difficult and expensive to make. Laptop screens use liquid crystals to form an image. These work in much the same way as the display on a digital watch.

external disk drives

printer

▶ Laptop computers have to squeeze everything into a small space. Instead of using a mouse, you can move your finger on a screen-shaped rubber pad.

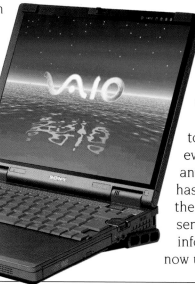

Keyed up

Information is typed into a computer using a keyboard. Pressing a key on a keyboard connects two metal contacts. This makes electric current flow, so the computer knows which key has been pressed.

A mouse makes a computer easier to use. Instead of having to type everything, you can point and click anywhere on the screen. A simple mouse has a ball inside it that rolls as you move the mouse around. Rollers around the ball sense the ball's movement, and pass this information to the computer. Some mice now use a laser instead of the ball.

▶ Computer screens based on CRTs are bulky and use a lot of power. Newer flat screens use low power but are very expensive.

flat-screen monitor

Hitting a key on the keyboard makes an electrical contact, which causes a signal to go to the computer. Microchips in the computer change the keyboard signals into letters on the screen.

keyboard

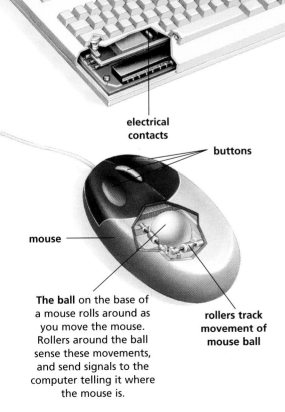

electrical contacts

buttons

mouse

The ball on the base of a mouse rolls around as you move the mouse. Rollers around the ball sense these movements, and send signals to the computer telling it where the mouse is.

rollers track movement of mouse ball

◀ A cutaway view of a computer and some 'peripherals': devices that are not part of the computer itself. Peripherals such as the keyboard are input devices: they feed information into the computer. Output devices, such as the screen and printer, display information from the computer. Parts such as disk drives are input/output (I/O) devices.

If you like computer games, you can plug in a joystick. This not only lets you steer, say, a starship around the screen, but it also has extra buttons that make games more fun.

Going for a spin

Disks are a good way of either storing data or taking it from one computer to another. There are two main types of disk. Magnetic disks, like a computer's hard drive or a floppy disk, store data as patterns of magnetism. Optical disks, like CDs or DVDs, store data (or music) in the form of tiny pits in the shiny surface. Optical disks can store hundreds, or even thousands of times more information than a floppy disk.

Disks store all sorts of things – including pictures. Digital cameras take pictures that are stored in memory chips or on a tiny floppy disk. They can be used directly in computer files. For pictures that already exist on paper, you can use a scanner to copy the image into the computer.

To get copies of documents out of the computer, you need a printer. Printers simply turn the text or pictures on the screen into tiny dots on paper. The dots can be made of ink or, in a laser printer, a powder called toner.

🔵 key words

- keyboard
- magnetic disk
- mouse
- optical disk
- screen

Microchips will soon be able to store as much data as a computer hard drive. So hard disks will one day be replaced by cards containing memory chips.

APPLICATIONS AND PROGRAMS

If you want to bake a really delicious chocolate cake, it's best to follow a recipe. If you follow the instructions carefully, the cake should be great! A computer program can also be thought of as a recipe. It is a list of instructions that makes the computer do the job you want it to.

▲ Electronic games have been popular since people first began making personal computers. Modern games have sophisticated graphics that can simulate whole environments.

Computer programs can do really useful things, like control a space rocket, manage your washing machine cycle or change the traffic lights.

A computer's programs are part of its software. The software of a computer is every bit as important as the hardware (the physical parts like the screen and keyboard). If the software is wrong, the program won't work – just like a recipe.

Home on the range

The range of software is staggering. We are all used to word processors, which let us type letters and get them right before we print them out or email them. But PCs can also run programs that let you store information (databases), programs that do calculations (spreadsheets), programs that

▼ There are many types of computer program. Some are lists of things to do, while others, like this one, describe how a web page should look. Web pages are usually written in Hyper Text Mark-up Language (HTML). The HTML code on the right makes the page shown on the left.

play music or sounds, ones that let you draw pictures or modify photographs – and of course computer games. There are also many other kinds of software used in science and industry.

One kind of program that has to be designed with extra care is safety-critical software. This is the software that operates aircraft, cars or medical equipment. If safety-critical software goes wrong, people can get hurt.

Not all software is useful. Computer viruses are pieces of software that invade computer systems and cause problems.

BILL GATES AND MICROSOFT

In the early 1980s, IBM designed a revolutionary computer, the IBM PC (personal computer). It was small enough to sit on a desk. But their computer had no software – so IBM turned to a tiny firm called Microsoft for help. This company was run by a young American called Bill Gates. Microsoft then wrote MS-DOS – the MicroSoft Disk Operating System – for the IBM PC. With every PC sold making money for Microsoft, the firm soon became a huge corporation, and is now the world's leading software maker.

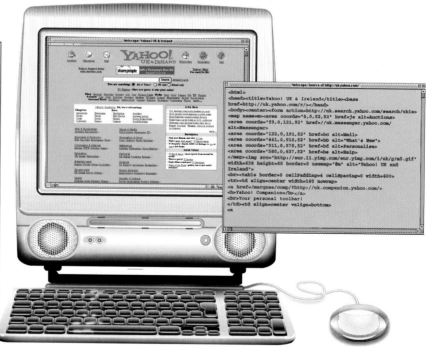

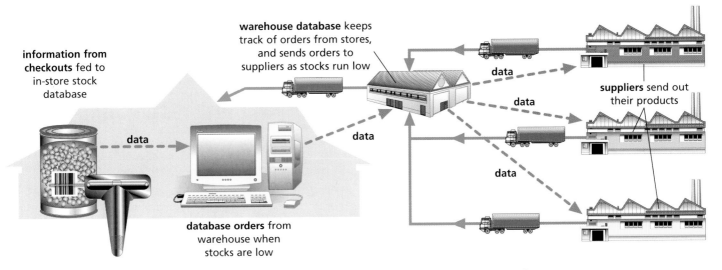

information from checkouts fed to in-store stock database

warehouse database keeps track of orders from stores, and sends orders to suppliers as stocks run low

data

suppliers send out their products

data

data

data

database orders from warehouse when stocks are low

Some viruses just display cheeky messages, while others erase certain types of file, like pictures or music files. Some viruses erase everything on your computer. Viruses are often spread by email. To fight them, it's important to have up-to-date anti-virus software that stops them working.

◀ Complex software is used to control much of the engine management, and even gear changes, in Formula One racing cars.

▲ Databases are important programs for many businesses. In a supermarket, databases keep track of what needs ordering at the store, at the warehouse, and at the supermarket's many suppliers.

key words

- application
- bug
- computer language
- computer virus
- database
- program
- software
- spreadsheet

Mind your language

Software is written in a computer language. There are many languages – BASIC, Java, and Fortran are a few examples. Each is good at different things. For example, BASIC is a simple language that beginners can learn. Java is a more complex language that makes Internet programs work on many different types of computer. Fortran is a more specialist scientific language. Programmers choose the language for the job in hand.

Some programs can be very long. The program that guides a space rocket into orbit, for instance, can be many thousands of lines long. That's because there are many different pieces of equipment to control, and many pieces of information that need including in the program.

Computer processors cannot understand programs directly. The words and figures in a program have to be converted first into digital instructions that the computer processor can understand. This is done using a system called a compiler.

Bugs and debugging

Because a program is a list of instructions, any mistake in the commands can stop the program working. This could be serious if the software is controlling, for example, the engines on an aeroplane or a computer that does blood tests. So errors, known to computer programmers as 'bugs', have to be removed. Debugging (getting rid of bugs) can take as long as writing the program in the first place.

A MATTER OF DESIGN

Animated movies like *Toy Story* and *A Bug's Life* were made entirely on computers. To make computer graphics appear to move naturally, a computer has to make about 24 pictures for every second of the movie. And each picture is made up of millions of coloured dots called pixels. This needs a lot of computing power.

It took about 35 years after the invention of computers for the technology to become good enough to make computer movies. But movies are only one of many areas where computers are being used to design things.

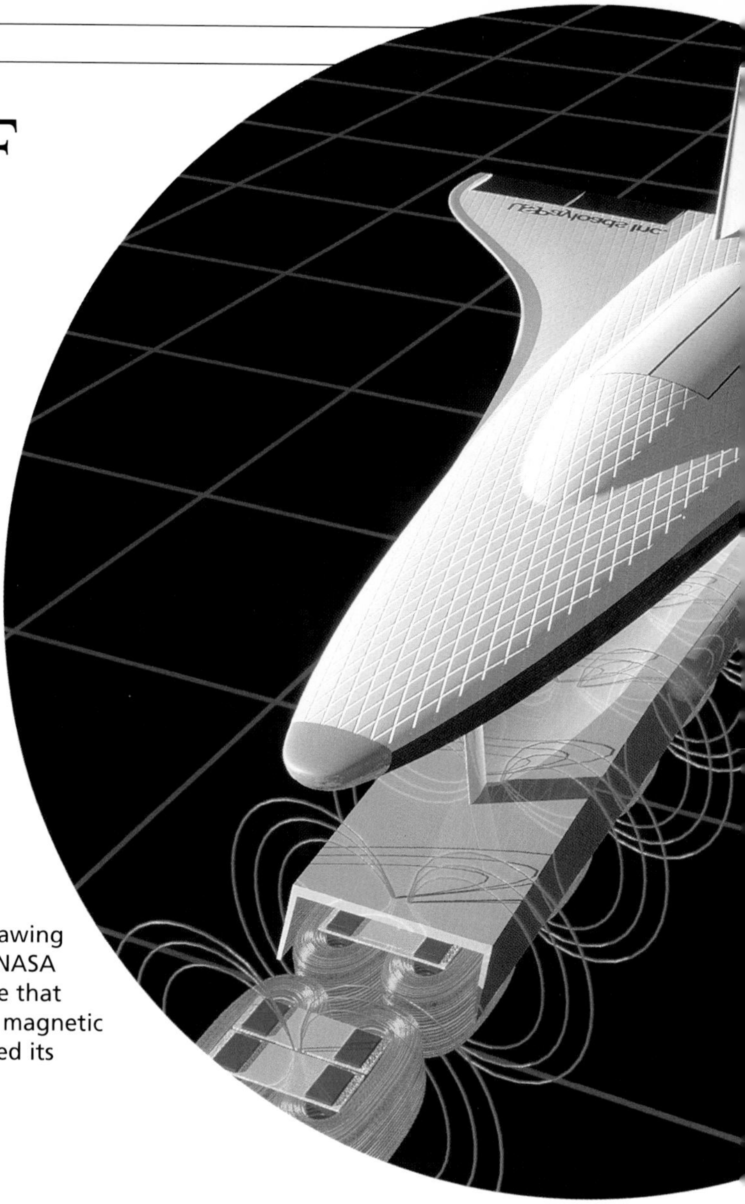

▶ A CAD drawing of a future NASA space shuttle that might use a magnetic track to speed its take off.

◀ The characters Woody and Buzz Lightyear from the *Toy Story* movies were created on computer. Extremely fast, powerful supercomputers are needed to create a full-length animated film.

key words

- Computer Aided Design (CAD)
- pixel
- simulator

Planes, trains and cars

If you travel in a car, train, bus or plane, the vehicle has almost certainly been designed on a computer. The same goes for bridges, buildings and even clothes.

There are many advantages to designing things on a computer. The main one is that you can try many different designs until you have one that is just right. And the computer can make sure that you use the least amount of material to make, say, a new style of jacket. So you save money.

What a CAD

Designing things with the help of computers is called Computer Aided Design (CAD). This takes advantage of the fact that it is easy to save pictures of things in a computer's memory.

Using a CAD system, drawings are made on the computer screen using a special pen that you press on a rectangular pad called a graphics tablet. This uses the pressure of the pen tip on the pad to draw on the computer screen. A mouse could also be used. But if you already have a hand-drawn picture of a car, you can use an image scanner to capture it on the computer.

The pixels (dots) that make up the drawing are saved as a number of digital 'bits' in the computer's memory and displayed on the computer's screen. The software then lets you do things like show the design from a different angle, or colour it differently. Designs drawn with a CAD system can be printed out as plans for making

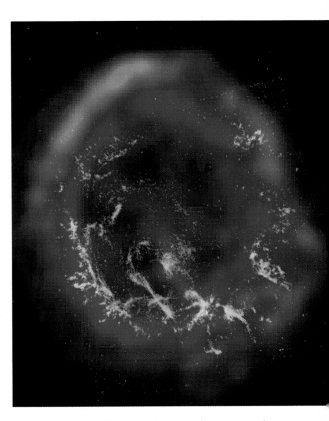

▶ Astronomers can use computers to put together information from different types of telescope into a single picture. In this picture of the remains of an exploded star, the blue parts came from an X-ray telescope, the green from an optical telescope and the red from a radio telescope.

▼ Engineers usually work out their designs in three dimensions, then produce plans on paper. But using rapid prototyping, they can now make solid models of objects from computerized plans. The printer works by building up the object in thousands of thin layers.

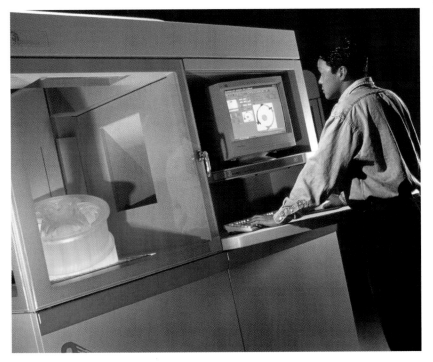

something, or they can be used to control the machines that are used to make the parts. With a technique called rapid prototyping, it is even possible to print out a solid, three-dimensional model of the object in rubber, wax, plastic, metal or a material similar to plywood.

Applying physics

But drawing is only part of the design. Computers also let you check, for example, how a bridge design will stand up to high winds or very low temperature. This is called simulation. Computer simulations save money, as engineers don't have to build the design to see how it behaves. If the simulation shows problems, they can be corrected before anything is built.

Simulation using computer graphics is also useful for teaching. Airline pilots 'fly' a computerized flight simulator before they fly a real plane.

Computer images also help scientists to understand things. Molecules are too small to see, but models of them can be drawn on computers and studied to see how they might be useful. And radio telescope images of space can be cleaned up so that far-off galaxies can be seen more clearly.

DATASPACE

You are in a building you have never been in before. You move into a room to explore it. But suddenly, the floor disappears and you are falling. Looking up as the room disappears above you, you see the blackness of space. This is the kind of experience that you can have when you enter the world of virtual reality.

Virtual reality (VR) involves creating a three-dimensional environment inside a computer's memory. It can be a room, a cave, or a shopping mall. The idea is to let people explore that space by looking around it and walking around it in as natural a way as possible, listening to sounds they might hear, even feeling things that they might touch. Virtual reality lets designers get a feel for buildings or cars that have not even been built yet. Players of computer games can use virtual reality to reach a new level of realism.

adjustable headpiece

tiny video screen (one for each eye)

lens system

surround-sound headphones

▶ VR helmets have a screen for each eye and surround-sound speakers. Sensors tell the computer when you move your head.

 key words

- graphics
- sensors
- virtual reality

In your head

To get you inside the 'space' in the computer, VR systems use a head-mounted display that contains two tiny computer monitors, one for each eye. The images are slightly different in each, to create a three-dimensional effect.

But the really clever thing about a VR helmet is that when your head moves, the graphics you see move too. Magnetic sensors in the helmet tell the computer how much you move, so it can change the image correspondingly. This makes you feel that you are in the environment. Speakers in the helmet let you hear sound all around you for added realism.

You can use a 'data glove' to help make VR even more authentic. When you 'push' on something, tiny balloons in the glove inflate, pressing on your hand. It feels like you've really pushed something!

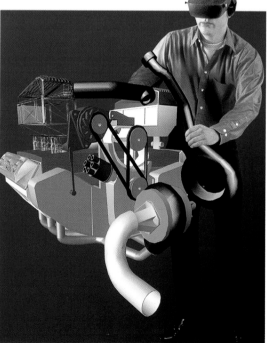

◀ Using VR, engineers can 'walk around' their design ideas, getting a sense of how they will look – and even feel – without having to build them. This picture shows an engineer with a virtual model of an engine.

Researchers are working on adding 'thought control' to VR systems. Using brainwave sensors inside a VR helmet, people will be able to control or change what they listen to, by just thinking about it.

SURFING THE WEB

The internet connects you to people, businesses and organizations all around the world. You can listen to faraway radio stations, download music from new bands, or play computer games. And you can find out almost anything you might want to know.

Few inventions have changed people's lives as much as the internet. Long-lost families have been reunited by it. Some people have found life-saving information on it. All these amazing developments have been made possible by a communications network that goes all over the world.

What is the internet?

The internet is a vast network of computers, connected to each other in a variety of ways. The original internet was a small computer network, set up in the 1960s by American military scientists who wanted a reliable way of communicating with each other in emergencies. The network soon grew, as scientists realized how useful it could be.

Many large organizations are connected directly into the internet. But smaller users, such as people with PCs at home, connect to organizations called Internet Service

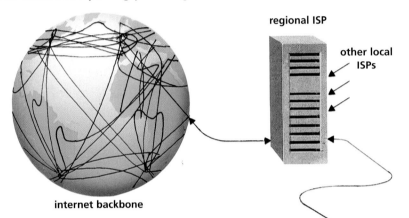

regional ISP

other local ISPs

internet backbone

company with small network

local ISP

home internet user

▲ Computers connect to the internet via an ISP. ISPs around the world are connected by the internet's 'backbones'. These are fibre-optic cables carrying information that span the globe.

▼ The internet is now available on some mobile phones. Accessing pages is slow, but phones are getting faster all the time.

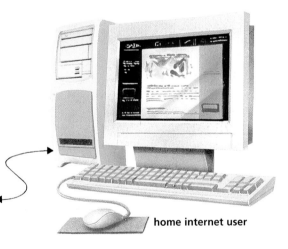

Providers (ISPs). The ISPs run special 'server' computers that pass on internet information.

Email and web pages

Sending messages by electronic mail (email) is one of the most popular things on the internet. All you need is a modem (a device that connects your computer to the telephone network) and an email program. You can write messages as long or as short as you like. And you can 'attach' all sorts of other computer files – a picture, a movie, a sound file or a computer program.

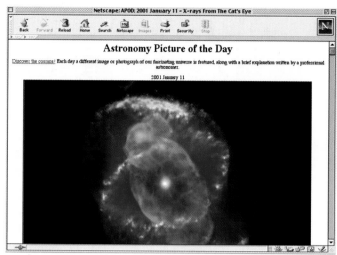

The internet also has billions of pages of information in the form of 'web' pages. To help you find your way around all this information, there are websites called search engines that help you find the pages you're interested in. If you are interested in dinosaurs, for instance, you can enter the word 'dinosaur', and the search engine will give you a list of sites on that subject.

Another very useful internet idea is the newsgroup. This lets people with a common interest send emails to whole

▲ How a search engine works. Suppose you want to find out about a website you have heard of, Astronomy Picture of the Day. Typing in 'astronomy picture of the day' gives a list of websites with these words in. And clicking on the first site in the list takes you to the website itself.

bunches of like-minded people. There are many thousands of such groups on an area of the internet called the usenet.

Internet shopping

The internet is also becoming important for business. Home shopping sites let you order groceries with an email and have them delivered. You need never go to a supermarket again.

But the net also threatens businesses such as record companies. A lot of music is now available on the internet, and people can make digital copies of songs and swap them for free. So bands and record companies constantly try to stop this 'piracy' happening.

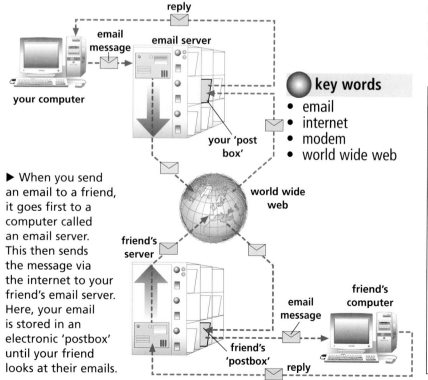

▶ When you send an email to a friend, it goes first to a computer called an email server. This then sends the message via the internet to your friend's email server. Here, your email is stored in an electronic 'postbox' until your friend looks at their emails.

key words
- email
- internet
- modem
- world wide web

THE WORLD WIDE WEB
The world wide web was invented to make scientists' lives easier. They needed a quick way of telling others around the world what research they were doing – and a quick way to see what research others were doing. So Tim Berners Lee (born 1955) and his colleagues at the European Particle Physics Laboratory (CERN) in Switzerland, invented the Hypertext Transfer Protocol (http). This makes it possible to look at pages of information from an Internet server on a PC. The web took off so fast after its launch in 1992 that it contained more than a billion pages by 2000.

INTELLIGENT MACHINES

'**S**hape shifter' robots can design themselves – and even recycle themselves. A computer designs the robot's parts, which are then 'printed out' by a machine called a 3-D printer. When the robot has finished the task it was built for, it melts itself down, and the plastic is used for another robot.

A robot is an automatic machine that does jobs under the control of its computer brain. The great advantage of a robot is that it doesn't make mistakes or get tired, and it can work just about anywhere.

Robot workers

Robots are used to do jobs that are too dangerous or boring for people to do. In factories, robots carry out tasks that have to be done over and over again, 24 hours a day. Robots are also used for dangerous tasks like getting broken or worn-out parts from nuclear reactors, or finding and disarming bombs.

The basic parts of a robot are a controller (the robot's 'brain'), sensors (these tell the robot about the outside world) and effectors (its 'hands').

▼ One way artificial intelligence researchers test out their ideas is to build robotic football players. But robot footballers aren't going to take over from humans for a while yet. Most games are decided by the number of own goals each team scores!

▼ The basic parts of a robot arm. Most robots will have pressure sensors – a sense of 'touch'. They might also have camera 'eyes', and microphone 'ears', or other non-human sensors like infrared vision. Most robots have an arm that can be fitted with several different effectors.

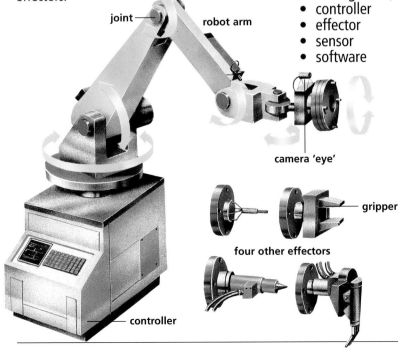

joint — robot arm

camera 'eye'

gripper

four other effectors

controller

key words
- artificial intelligence (AI)
- controller
- effector
- sensor
- software

Smart and smarter

A robot making things in a factory can be 'trained' by a human operator. It learns by copying the movements the human makes. But robots of this type are limited to doing only a handful of tasks.

Artificial intelligence (AI) researchers are now trying to make robots more clever, so that they can do a wider range of jobs. A major aim is to build robots that can work out for themselves how to do things. Experimental robots have been made that can learn and 'evolve' new ways of doing tasks.

Soon, robots will be in our living rooms. A vacuum cleaner that can wander around a room on its own, sucking up dust and dirt, is being developed. But because trailing a power cord might trip people up, it is battery powered.

GLOSSARY

This glossary gives simple explanations of difficult or specialist words that readers might be unfamiliar with. Words in *italic* have their own glossary entry.

AC Alternating Current. Electric *current* that flows first one way around a *circuit*, and then the other way. The mains electricity in homes is AC.

battery A device for storing *electricity*, until it is needed, in the form of chemical energy. Also known as a *cell*.

capacitor Part of a *circuit* that stores *electrons* (charge) between two metal plates. The plates are usually rolled up inside a cylinder.

cell Another name for a *battery* (or a single part of a battery).

circuit A conducting wire loop that allows *electrons* to travel around it. On the way, the electrons do useful jobs, such as making a light bulb glow.

computer A machine that stores and processes information (data) under the control of a list of instructions called a *program*.

conductor A substance, such as a metal, that allows an electric *current* to flow through it.

current Measure of the rate at which electric charge (*electrons*) flow around a *circuit*. Measured in amperes, often shortened to 'amps'.

DC Direct Current. DC flows in only one direction around a circuit. *Batteries* provide DC.

digital Of a computer, representing information as a series of numbers consisting only of 1s and 0s.

electricity A form of energy carried by certain particles of matter (*electrons* and protons), used for lighting and heating and for making machines work.

electromagnetic induction The production of an electric *current* in a *circuit* when the circuit is placed in a changing *magnetic field*. Electricity *generators* use induction to make electricity.

electromagnetic radiation A kind of radiation that is made up of waves, including radio waves, visible light and X-rays.

electron A tiny negatively charged particle in orbit around the nucleus (centre) of an atom. Some electrons are free to move, creating electric *current*.

email (electronic mail) Messages sent and received electronically, between *computers* that are linked by the *internet*.

generator A machine that produces electric *current*. Generators in power stations produce alternating current (*AC*). They are driven by giant turbines that are powered by steam (in coal, oil and nuclear power stations) or by water (in hydroelectric power stations).

hard disk A spinning magnetic disc on which *computers* record (save) and retrieve (open) data files.

insulator A substance, such as rubber, that blocks the flow of electric *current*.

internet A global *computer* network connected by satellites, optical fibres and telephone wires.

magnet A substance in which *electrons* spin in one direction, creating a *magnetic field*. Similar ends of magnets will push away (repel) each other; different ends will attract each other.

magnetic field A region around magnets, magnetic materials and current-carrying conductors, where a magnetic force is present.

memory chip A microchip in which digital data is stored until needed.

microchip A chip of silicon containing a complex *circuit* made of thousands of microscopic *transistors*, *capacitors* and *resistors*. They use very little power and work extremely fast because the parts are very close together.

microprocessor A *microchip* that performs simple calculations on computer data, at lightning-fast speeds. Microprocessors contain many millions of *transistors*, but are no bigger than a thumbnail.

program The list of instructions, or software, followed by a *computer's* hardware. Usually supplied on a floppy disk, CD or DVD, but may also be downloaded from the *internet*.

resistance A measure of how hard it is to push a *current* through a substance. Measured in ohms.

resistor Part of a *circuit* that resists the flow of *current*, causing a voltage (electrical pressure) to be raised across it.

switch Part of a *circuit* that opens and closes like a gate, letting *electrons* flow only when you want them to.

transformer Part of a *circuit* that either increases or decreases the size of an *AC* signal.

transistor Part of a *circuit* that either boosts (amplifies) a signal or turns it on and off to represent *digital* data in *computers*.

transmitter Equipment used to produce and send signals as *electromagnetic* waves (radiation). Transmitters are used to send radio waves to radio and television aerials.

volt Measure of the electrical pressure (potential difference) in a *circuit*. This pressure urges *electrons* to flow.

watt Measure of the power produced or consumed by a *circuit*.

world wide web A part of the *internet* that helps users to find information by providing links between documents.

INDEX

Page numbers in **bold** mean that this is where you will find the most information on that subject. If both a heading and a page number are in bold, there is an article with that title. A page number in *italic* means that there is a picture of that subject. There may also be other information about the subject on the same page.

ACKNOWLEDGEMENTS

Key
t = top; c = centre; b = bottom; r = right; l = left; back = background; fore = foreground

Artwork
Baker, Julian: 20 tr. **D'Achille, Gino:** 4 tr; 9 bl; 11 tr; 13 tr; 23 bl; 24 br; 35 br; 38 bl; 44 br. **Franklin, Mark:** 18 cr, b; 19 tr; 27 b. **Full Steam Ahead:** 23 bc; 32 tr; 38 br. **Gecko Ltd.:** 15 bl. **Jakeway, Rob:** 39 tr; 44 bl. **Parsley, Helen:** 42 tr. **Saunders, Michael:** 12 tr, c; 16 bl; 21 b; 30 br; 34–35 b; 43 c; 45 bl. **Smith, Guy (Mainline Design):** 5 tc; 7c; 8 tr; 9 bc; 10 tr, bl; 13 cr; 24 bl; 26 cl; 28–29 tc; 36–37 c. **Sneddon, James:** 8 br; 14 tr; 29 b. **Visscher, Peter:** 4 tl; 7 tl; 8 tl; 10 tl; 12 tl; 14 tl; 15 tl; 16 tl; 18 tl; 20 tl; 22 tl, b; 24 tl; 24–25 c; 26 tl, bl; 27 tl; 28 tl; 30 tl; 31 tl; 31–32 b; 34 tl; 36 tl; 38 tl; 42 tl; 43 tl; 45 tl.

Photos
The publishers would like to thank the following for permission to use their photographs.

3 d Systems Europe Ltd.: 41 bl.
BBC: 29 tr.
Bubbles Photo Library: 5 br (Loisjoy Thurstun).
C Technologies AB: 33 tr.
Corbis: 12 bl (David Samuel); 17 bl (Bettmann); 38 tr (Jim Sugar Photography).
Eon Productions: 30 cl (Jim Clark/Avid Technology).
Ford: 9 tc.
Google Inc.: 44 tl.
Hutchison Picture Library: 27 tr (Christina Dodwell).
Intel Corporation: 34 tr.
Kobal: 40 bl, tl (Disney Enterprises).
Lego: 15 cr.
NASA: 8 bl; 41 tr (NASA/CXC/SAO; NASA/HST (optical); CSIRO/ATNF/ATCA (radio)).

Nokia: 25 cr; 43 bl.
Oxford Scientific Films: 4 b (Warren Faidley); 7 bl (David M. Dennis).
Philips: 21 cl, c.
Psion: 31 cr.
Science Photo Library: 6 tr (BSIP VEM); 6 cl (Blair Seitz); 7 tr (Chris Knapton); 11 b (Rosenfeld Images Ltd.); 12–13 c (Alex Bartel); 14 bl (Peter Menzel); 16 tr (Martin Bond); 17 tr (John Mead); 19 bl; 20 bl (Tony Craddock); 21 tr (Sandia National Laboratories); 22 bl (TEK Image); 28 bl; 35 tr (B. Kramer/Custom Medical Stock Photo); 39 bl (Philippe Plailly/Eurelios); 40–41 tc (NASA); 42 bl (Geoff Tompkinson); 45 cr (Volker Steger).
Sony: 36 bl; 37 br.
Sony UK Ltd.: 21 cr; 30 tr.
Virgin Atlantic Airways: 31 b.
Woodfall Wild Images: 23 c (Paul Kay).